SLIPPERY

ACKNOWLEDGE AND OVERCOME
THE DOWNFALLS THAT KEEP US FROM
LIVING OUR BEST LIVES

SLOPES

KAREN (BALYEAT) THOMPSON

AND
ANTIDOTES

WESTBOW
PRESS®
A DIVISION OF THOMAS NELSON
& ZONDERVAN

WestBow Press books may be ordered through booksellers or by contacting:

WestBow Press
A Division of Thomas Nelson & Zondervan
1663 Liberty Drive
Bloomington, IN 47403
www.westbowpress.com
844-714-3454

ISBN: 979-8-3850-0589-5 (sc)
ISBN: 979-8-3850-0590-1 (e)

Library of Congress Control Number: 2023916222

Print information available on the last page.

WestBow Press rev. date: 09/21/2023

DEDICATION

Never underestimate the impact you can have on someone's life. Max, Thyra, Wayne, and Opal all lived lives worthy of modeling. Each one played a pivotal part in my spiritual journey. Some of them have passed away, but their impact lives on. They all displayed two very admirable qualities: integrity and consistency.

Max taught our young adult Sunday school class when Duane and I were newly married. Many of our lifelong friendships were formed during those early years of our marriage. Max had a way of bringing people together and sharing wisdom from God's Word. It was such a positive experience for us. Max was compassionate, humble, and vulnerable. He didn't hesitate to share some of the downfalls or slippery slopes that he encountered. His teachings were relevant. He often shared from his own life experiences. He could cry and laugh with us. His character, humor, and leadership were the right balance for so many of us young adults just trying to find our way. The deepest impression he made on me was seeing the consistency in his life. He was also president of Crown International for many years; I worked down the hall from Max for five of those years. I admired his character. He was the same Monday–Friday as he was on Sunday morning. Max passed away at the age of sixty-six.

Thyra is the kind of person you want in your corner. She is one of the kindest, sweetest, and godliest women I've ever been blessed to know. Grace and wisdom are beautifully woven into her life. I was honored and blessed to sit with Thyra on our church deacon board for several years. She never planned without prayerful and thoughtful consideration.

Wayne was my pastor for many years. I never had to second-guess him. He was always the same unless there was a sporting competition involved. He was strong in his convictions, sincere, trustworthy, and humble. He showed his congregation how to step away from a position with integrity when it was time to pass the torch. Wayne will go down as one of the finest men I've ever known.

Opal was my mentor. She had an aura about her that portrayed great confidence. She was a strong woman of faith. During our mentoring sessions, she would assure me that she did not have all the answers but that she would provide me with guidance and support. Our conversations flowed with ease. She was exactly what I needed at a very fragile time in my life. She was a great encourager. Opal passed away in February 2018. She was eighty-four years old.

Sometimes, it's upon reflection that we learn the value of a relationship and how deeply it has enriched us. Max, Thyra, Wayne, and Opal did not hide behind their personal "slippery slopes." Instead, they were vulnerable. There was no pretense or facade. How refreshing!

CONTENTS

Introduction...xi

Chapter 1   Stand Up to the Storm 1
Chapter 2   The Blame Game 17
Chapter 3   Buyer Beware 31
Chapter 4   The Race of Your Life 45
Chapter 5   What Are You So Afraid Of?...................55
Chapter 6   Lighten Up!..................................67
Chapter 7   Dust Off Your Lenses......................... 79
Chapter 8   Where's God in All of This? 91
Chapter 9   Leave Your Pride at the Door................103
Chapter 10 Personal Blind Spots.........................111
Chapter 11 Wait a Minute! I Can Fix That!...........121
Chapter 12 Put on the Final Touches....................127

Notes 133

INTRODUCTION

I love to watch Alpine skiing during the Winter Olympics. I can sit in a comfortable chair in my living room and be entertained by the results of their hard work, training, and endurance. Honestly, I do not even think about the preparation they went through while watching the event. I just sit back and enjoy a cup of hot cocoa with a nice warm blanket draped over my lap. Let the games begin!

Once the advertisement is over and the announcer has made the introduction, the skier approaches the top of the hill. They take one last glance at the snow-covered course in front of them. They position themselves for the run. Their knees are slightly bent. Ski poles are in each hand for balance and building momentum on the way down. They start the race with a strong push-off, gaining speed as they go down the mountain slope as quickly as possible.

They meticulously glide around each pylon with technical precision as the snow sprays into the air. It is astounding to watch them! It's a beautiful event when everything goes as planned and the skiers are happy with their time. But if you watch the event enough, you will witness times when the skiers lose control and they totally wipe out. Their skis go flying up in the air as they tumble and fall on the icy slope. Once they gather themselves, they carefully stand up and walk off the course. They often glance up at the fans to give a friendly wave, signaling that they are OK.

The truth is they are devastated! That friendly wave signals "I'm OK" on the outside, but there's a lot of frustration and disappointment going on inside of them. They do not give up because they took a tumble. In fact, they have taken many tumbles. They did not get to the Olympics without going through a lot of physical and emotional pain. They got to the Olympics because they never gave up. They are a part of the one percent of athletes who make it to the pros.

Our lives are full of slippery slopes. They are the things in life that cause us to stumble, fall, and wipe out. Every now and then, an avalanche comes up behind us, building momentum and knocking us off balance. We feel buried under the heaviness of it all.

If we allow the slippery slopes in life to get the best of us, we'll stay defeated because, sometimes, it's just too hard to get back up on our own. But like the determined athletes, we need to press on until we get it right. The athletes know they've worked too hard to give up.

Our lives are standing on top of the hill. We know there is a lot at risk. We have tried to prepare, but there are always those moments that catch us off guard—poor weather conditions or the course is not as prepped as it should be or we are just not on our best game. Whatever it is, we must get our balance, get back up, and try again.

For every slippery slope, there is an antidote. Life is just too precious to let the slopes get the best of us. The topics I have chosen to write about are some of the biggest hurdles I have had to face and overcome in my life. This is a victory story! There are answers to the struggles we face.

The people I dedicated this book to are a small sampling of those who have personally taught me how to overcome some major hurdles in my life. Let us look at each slippery slope knowing that there is an antidote to help us live our best lives.

CHAPTER 1

STAND UP TO THE STORM

Jesus Said, "Peace, Be Still."

I have told you these things, so that you may
have peace. In this world you will have trouble.
But take heart! I have overcome the world.
—John 16:33 (NIV)

The Author and Perfecter of our lives is a holy God, yet
He never painted a picture of perfection for this side of
eternity. He is noticeably clear! "In this world, you will
have trouble." Our heavenly Father warns us that trouble
is coming our way. Like any good father, He knows
when to initiate the conversation. He wants us to know
how to defend ourselves when we get into trouble. We
need our heavenly Father on speed dial!

If our earthly father failed to communicate the escape plan for staying out of trouble, that does not mean he did not love us. It might mean he did not know how to start the conversation. My father did not give me a lot of earthly advice, but he was a good example. He was far from perfect, but he knew how to have fun, forgive, and not hold grudges. He knew how to love people, and he loved Jesus!

Our heavenly Father is a great communicator! He's timely, appropriate, and patient. He is gracious, compassionate, slow to anger, and rich in love. He's not swayed, intimidated, or fearful! He will stand up against the hardest-hitting storms and win every time. We need Him on our side and in our corner.

Jesus was spontaneous! His disciples had to be on their toes, ready to listen to and follow the sound of His voice. They had to learn how to be flexible. When Jesus said, "Let's go," they went. When Jesus told them to "stay behind," that is what they did, willingly or not. One evening, Jesus said to His disciples, "Let's cross to the other side of the lake." So the disciples got into the boat with Him, and they began to cross the lake, leaving the crowds behind. Jesus was tired from the events of the day, so He went to the stern of the boat to take a nap.

He had been with people all day, and He needed rest. He may have also wanted to escape the drama that His disciples could often engage in.

The boat was about twenty-seven feet long, and Jesus didn't have earbuds to block out all the chatter. It was not like a cruise ship where we can go to our private cabins to get away from it all. The boat was a bit crowded, so Jesus had to settle for a less than ideal place to sleep. His disciples seemed content just rowing along. Being on the water was familiar territory for them, as many of them had grown up as anglers by trade. Conversations were flowing, and all was going well when, suddenly, out of nowhere, dark storm clouds rolled in, and a violent storm struck the lake. They had no warning. There was no time to prepare. The high and powerful waves demanded control, rocking the boat from side to side. Every wave gained more strength and power, splashing furiously over the sides of the boat. It is one thing to be in the middle of the sea in daylight, but when a storm strikes at night, it adds a whole new dimension to the experience.

The disciples were overwhelmed as they scrambled to get control. Their eyes and bodies were drenched in lake water and rain. Their hands were wet and slippery, making it hard to row. They could barely see from the heavy mist. They wiped their faces but had no relief from the wind and the rain. Everything seemed out of control! Through their blurred vision, their eyes scanned the boat for Jesus. Where did He go? As they caught a glimpse of Him lying down, they wondered how He could sleep through this. Did He not realize what was going on? Could He not hear the crashing thunder or feel the boat hitting the waves or hear their cries of desperation? Who was this Jesus that He could sleep so calmly through a storm?

Out of frustration and fear for their lives, they called out to Him, "Lord, save us! We're going to drown!" In their minds, the only one who could save them had fallen asleep. Have you ever felt that way—abandoned by the only one who should be there for you?

After the disciples cried out in search for Jesus, He replied, "Why are you so afraid? You have so little faith!" Then He got up and rebuked the winds and the waves, and, suddenly, there was a great calm. The men in the boat were amazed and asked, "What kind of man is this that even the winds and the waves obey Him?"

Jesus could have spoken calm into the storm from any physical position, but scripture says "He got up and rebuked the winds and the waves." He was showing the disciples how to speak with authority because there will be times when God calls us to be active participants in the calming of our own storms. When we sit back and do nothing, the waves overtake us. After Jesus calmed the storm, He talked to His disciples like any good father talks to his child when he wants to make a crucial point. I don't know about you, but I would have felt like crawling into a hole. I hear rebuke in His words: "Why are you so afraid? You have so little faith!" His words are the same today. Why is our faith so small?

A disturbance like the storm can suck the life out of us. When all seems hopeless, it does not matter how many people are in the boat with us. The *Titanic* had over two thousand people on board; however, that brought them no comfort when faced with their own fate. They were all vulnerable to something they had no control over.

Jesus had, and still has, lofty expectations for His followers. The disciples were young men and new believers, yet Jesus wanted them to get it; He wanted them to know He could be trusted. He wanted them to know that they, too, had the power to calm the storm. Too many times we let the waves and the wind control us when God is only a prayer away. Prayer is our means to communicate with God. He hears the prayers of His children. If you do not have a relationship with God, this would be a good time to start one.

Those young disciples had a lot to learn, and Jesus was teaching them every day. Sometimes, He had to go over the same lesson repeatedly. But He saw their potential and never gave up on them. He will do the same for us when we follow Him.

Oftentimes, the storms in our lives blindside us, just like the storm did the disciples. Anything that breaks our hearts and brings pain is an unwanted disturbance— an onset of depression, job loss, bankruptcy, sickness, a wayward child, addiction, an unfulfilled marriage, poor test results, the loss of a loved one, or significant friendship. The list is long.

It's easy to talk about snowstorms, thunderstorms, or anything weather related. But when it comes to our personal storms, we often hide behind them or deny they even exist. We hope that, in time, they'll miraculously go away and no one will have noticed how badly we were hurting.

Exposure to storms can blind our eyes and rock our boats. When I was going through depression, all I wanted to do was sleep and hide. It never entered my mind to expose my emotional pain. No one wants to share feelings that make them vulnerable, weak, raw, and unguarded. Sadly, it would have been easier to tell someone I had a terminal illness than to admit depression. That unwanted disturbance in my life taught me understanding and empathy for those who are struggling with mental illness. I no longer express a worthless quick-fix remedy because it is just not that simple. The most difficult trials in life rarely have an easy answer, but there is always a lesson to be learned.

Mental illness is just one example of a storm that can rock our world and those around us. Every person deserves to know they are loved and not alone. We need to spread hope, not despair. I pray God opens our hearts and minds to see that mental illness is no more of a choice for someone than having cancer. God, help us all to be more kind, patient, and understanding.

As we put our faith in God, He opens our eyes to the world around us. We become more outwardly focused than inwardly focused. We begin to see how He is at work. God Knows the forecast and every storm that is brewing in our lives. We ask Him to prepare us, to give us strength and courage so we can stand firm against any disturbance, because storms make us fragile.

Duane and I live in northern Indiana, and we have seen how the power of wind can pull the roots of a decades-old oak tree right out of the ground and expose its foundation. It is an amazing picture of power—a strong and steady tree toppled over like a fragile tumbleweed. We cannot become complacent, thinking our roots are deep enough. Some difficulties in life leave us feeling damaged.

On Palm Sunday, April 11, 1965, my parents took me and my siblings to church like any other Sunday. As we sat through the evening service that night, we began to hear the loud sounds of rolling thunder and heavy wind. The rain was beating against the heavy etched-glass windowpanes, making it hard to concentrate. As a twelve-year-old, it was hard enough to concentrate in church. This storm brought the challenge to a new level. The whole congregation began to look around at one another with concern. The sounds were threatening!

As we left church that evening, the sky was hazy with colors of green and yellow. I had never seen the sky look so mysterious. When our family returned home from church, we dialed into a local weather station for an update. It wasn't long until all we could hear was the sound of sirens one right after another. It was like a nonstop alarm that had us all feeling on edge, scared, and nervous. It was a fear of the unknown. What was going on out there? We soon learned that a tornado had touched down not too far from us. What I did not understand about tornadoes was the uncanny stillness in the air right before it struck. That is where we get the saying "the calm before the storm."

Earlier that day when it appeared to be silent outside, there was a storm preparing for war. The wind and rain had been sucked into a funnel cloud like a vacuum cleaner, giving the cloud tremendous force. Is there a metaphor here? When we hold dreadful things inside, we can become like a funnel cloud, full of debris that can inflict pain, and destruction on ourselves and those closest to us. The strength of the Palm Sunday tornado had enough speed and force to drive a piece of straw from a farmer's field straight through a telephone pole. The straw was visible from both sides of the pole. Imagine that!

When we woke up on that Palm Sunday morning, it was a beautiful day! No one could have predicted the turn of events that would take place in just a matter of hours. Wind is a mystery! Like the power behind a storm, our biggest threats cannot always be seen. Many of the storms we encounter have nothing to do with the weather. On September 11, 2001, nineteen militants associated with the Islamic extremist group al-Qaeda hijacked four airplanes in the United States and carried out suicide attacks against specific targets. Almost three thousand people were killed that day. Those of us who lived through that frightening day will never forget where we were and how we felt.

I was at work that day like so many others. Once my coworkers and I heard the tragic news, we stood around in shock, wondering what this meant for our country and how it would end. Our management team realized our hearts and minds were too distraught to focus on work. We needed time to process what happened. They called us together for prayer. Nothing else mattered.

The world came to a standstill as air traffic controllers guided five thousand aircraft to the ground for safe landing in the matter of two hours. Airspace had to be cleared as no one knew if there were more attacks on the way. Those on airplanes were frantically notifying loved ones because they were uncertain of their plight. This storm was no longer brewing! This well-thought-out evil plan had been orchestrated methodically. Two of the four planes struck the Twin Towers of the World

Trade Center in New York City; the third plane hit the Pentagon in Arlington, Virginia; and the fourth plane crashed to the ground in Shanksville, Pennsylvania, before targeting Washington, DC.

A few brave passengers on Flight 93 took down the assailant before the final mission could be completed. It is times like this we scratch our heads and wonder, "What on earth is going on?" What evil did not realize that day is how fast our country would pull together, how hurt and despair turned into hope and strength, how unity was formed from all social classes and political parties.

As Americans, we proved ourselves unselfish and strong! We will forever be thankful for the men and women in uniform who took action to save lives and comfort so many. We hope and pray to never see another day like 9/11.

In a world of uncertainties, God knows what's coming! He's not surprised, caught off guard, shocked, or bewildered. He is not sitting on the throne wondering what to do next. He is completely self-sufficient! He is trustworthy! God is not waiting on the next publication of the *Wall Street Journal* to see what just happened. He knows exactly what, when, where, and how. He is omniscient (all knowing), omnipotent (all powerful), and omnipresent (everywhere at the same time). Our finite minds will never comprehend His abilities. He simply calls us to follow Him into the boat and then trust Him when the storms arise.

"Peace, be still." Three simple words with so much power! Every day, a storm is brewing that has nothing to do with the weather. Trusting in the power of the almighty God will set us free from fear. The biggest downfall of the disciples was their lack of faith. Are we any different? When challenging times come our way and we are not getting answers, it's easy to doubt and wonder, but fear and faith cannot reside together. It's an oxymoron. It is like light and darkness, sadness and joy, or danger and safety. We either have one or the other.

The disciples called for Jesus in their fear. He was their 911 call. Jesus heard their shaky voices and saw the fear in their eyes. He spoke directly to the storm, and it obeyed Him! What Jesus wanted His disciples to learn that day was that they, too, could calm the storm if they had only believed.

We won't escape tough times. There will be seasons when sadness, loss, or disappointment overwhelms us. When we cannot find answers to problematic questions, it may feel like a tornado just sucked everything out of us. Tears roll off our pillows at night, but God sees our pain. He understands!

There have been times in my life when I wondered why God didn't respond to my prayers. Why didn't He suddenly calm the storm? Had He fallen asleep and forgotten about me? When we do not get quick answers, there's a reason for it. Over the fifty years of my Christian walk, my faith has been up and down. I have been strong, and I have been weak. The important part of my faith journey is that I always returned to God. It is when we continue to stray from Him that we forfeit a peaceful and fruitful life.

I chose to follow Jesus at the age of twenty-one. He is my Lord and Shepherd. But like a dumb and foolish sheep, I often strayed away. The alternate path looked pretty appealing at times. But dumb and foolish sheep do that ... they easily stray away. If not for God, those years would have been wasted.

Our choice is simple: Will we focus on the storm or the Storm Changer? Faith is hard! The answer, purpose, or reason is not always clear to us. Our faith is not based on what we can see; it is based on the one who sees everything, knows everything, and has it all under control. Faith is believing even when we don't understand.

How is your faith in God? On a scale from 1 to 10, is your faith an unwavering ten? Is it a five, right there in the middle, based on your circumstances? Is it a one or two because you've never allowed God to speak into your life? You have kept him at a distance, only allowing a little space for Him, but when the storm starts to brew in your life, then you invite him in? Our faith journey can be a slippery slope. When we fail to put our trust in God, we are on our own. Things can happen abruptly to get our attention or to grow us in our faith. Whatever the purpose or cause, storms are always an unwanted disturbance. They demand our attention, and they cannot be ignored!

I have come to realize that no matter what I go through in life, there's a reason and purpose behind it, and I do not want to miss it. The antidote to our struggle is to put our trust in God. Once we comprehend how much He loves us, it will become second nature for us to turn to Him for wisdom and comfort. We will be able to lay our burdens and cares at his feet knowing He has our best interest at heart.

When life is going well, we can get lackadaisical. We can go along day after day not giving much thought to our lives until something gets our attention, something happens that shakes us to the core of our being, causing everything to come to a halt. Don't wait for a storm to brew to call upon the name of the Lord. He will use our good times to prepare us for the tough times. It is like taking a spiritual antioxidant. Draw near to God, and He will draw nearer to us.

Tonight, as you lay our head on your pillow, ask God to give you His peace no matter what you're going through. He sees you, and He understands. He loves you, and He cares for you more than anyone. As parents, we know how important it is to have our children trust us. We work on that relationship. But, sure enough, there will be a day when we must decide to protect our child in a way that they will not like or understand. But if we are good parents, our love and logic will win out even when our children do not get it or understand. We always do what is best for them. God is the same! He always does what is best for us even when we do not get it or understand. Trust can be hard, but it is our best option.

Almighty Father,

I thank You for loving me. I need You to be in the driver's seat of my life every minute of every day. Forgive me for the times I have settled for less than Your best because I have tried to manage the storm on my own terms. When I face an unwanted disturbance, give me the faith and confidence to be strong and patient. I believe in You and desire to walk with You all the days of my life. I know there are storms brewing that I know nothing about. I am asking You to give me strength and wisdom as the storms approach. Help me understand the test and to learn and grow from it. You are worthy of my trust.

In Jesus's name,

Amen

CHAPTER 2

THE BLAME GAME

God Set the Record Straight

Yes, each of us will give a personal account to God.
—Romans 14:12 (NLT)

Sooner or later, we will all have to face God,
regardless of our conditions. We will appear
before Christ and take what is coming to us as
a result of our actions, either good or bad.
—2 Corinthians 5:10 (The Message)

I do not like the sound of judgment any more than
anyone else. The word is cringeworthy. We equate it to
being harsh, critical, opinionated, or threatening. No
one wants to be judged! We fear the judge will not be
fair, objective, or have our best interest at heart. But on

the day of God's judgment, He will be fair for sure! You see, God is perfect. He does not have any motives or self-interest. He knows all things pure and simple. On judgment day, we will be standing face-to-face with a Holy and Omnipotent God. We cannot run or hide. We won't be able to blame anyone for our choices.

Blame has become the great diversion. We see it in politics, the government, families, and relationships. It's a game everyone participates in at some point, but no one really likes it because no one wins. It makes us feel better temporarily, but it does not change the outcome. We learn to play it at an early age, and we play it often.

We find it easy to justify ourselves and blame others. Our behavior becomes a *slippery slope* when we fail to take responsibility for our own actions. On the day of judgment, the buck stops with everyone being accountable for our own lives. That should cause all of us to pause and reflect on the day that awaits us all.

There was a day when I was running low on patience. It happens! I was in a hurry at the grocery store, and I only had a few items in my handheld basket. I thought to myself, *I should be able to get out of here in no time.* Then I looked and saw that someone with a cartful of groceries was in the only "fast" checkout lane available where the sign clearly reads "Limit 20 items."

That person clearly did not know how to follow the rules! As I tapped my foot and waited impatiently, I showed disdain on my face, giving them the stink eye. I hope they notice their rudeness! They never looked my way, so I could not have the satisfaction of shaming them. Then I was late for an appointment. The speed limit was 30 mph, but to make up time, I accelerated to 45 mph. It is so convenient to justify my choices and actions while blaming others when they inconvenience me or get in my way. We change the rules to fit our agenda. We do it without even thinking about it. Young people blame old people for being too slow. Old people blame young people for being too careless. Parents blame their kids for being on their phones too much, while they fail to set an example of restraint themselves. It's just so easy to do, and it's been going on since the beginning of creation.

The first example of the blame game is found in Genesis. The first man and first woman started it! Let us look at their story. Out of all of God's creations, only the woman was pleasing for Adam. That might be worth repeating. "The lord placed the man, Adam, in the garden to tend and watch over it." But God warned him, "You may freely eat the fruit of every tree in the garden except the tree of the knowledge of good and evil. If you eat its fruit, you are sure to die" (Gen. 2:15–17 [NLT]).

He warned Adam about the *one* tree that would hurt him! Isn't it just like us to want the one thing we cannot have? Is it curiosity or willful disobedience? Since Adam was appointed as groundskeeper of the garden, that made God his boss. Everything was perfect. Talk about pressure! Adam showed up every day for work, and Eve was close by.

Today, it might sound like this: Adam and Eve wake up and head to the kitchen to enjoy a cup of brew. They check the weather app and see that it's going to be a beautiful day. Adam says to Eve, "Hey, honey, how about we take a walk through the garden?" Eve gives Adam a thumbs up, and off they go barefoot, naked, and unashamed to the most amazing garden created by God. As they enter the garden, their eyes can hardly behold the beauty around them. The earthly sounds and fragrances capture their senses. It is like nothing they have ever experienced. The trees are of every size and shape and color. They observed the pure and peaceful river that flows throughout the garden supplying water to every living thing. This is surely a place to take friends to or sit on a park bench to read a favorite book. This place is serene and breathtaking!

As they walk deeper into the garden, Eve hears a voice from the serpent, "Did God really say you must not eat the fruit from any of the trees in the garden?" Who could have predicted the voice of the serpent to show up in such a beautiful location?

Lesson 1

Evil can show up in the most unexpected places and in some of the most unexpected people.

Genesis 3:1—Eve says to the serpent, "Of course we may eat fruit from the trees in the garden. It's only the fruit from the tree in the middle of the garden that we are not allowed to eat." She continues telling the serpent, "God said, 'You must not eat it or even touch it; if you do, you will die.'" She knew the rules!

God was not talking about a physical death; He was talking about a spiritual death. The serpent responds, "You won't die! God knows that your eyes will be opened as soon as you eat it, and you will be like God, knowing both good and evil." Eve starts to question herself when the serpent challenged her. He had planted a seed of doubt in her mind that she hadn't thought about before. The last thing she needed was the advice of a slithering snake. But it was not Eve's doubting that was sinful; it was her willful act of disobedience that allowed evil to prevail. "The woman was convinced. She saw that the tree was beautiful and its fruit looked delicious, and she wanted the wisdom it would give her. So, she took some of the fruit and ate it. Then she gave some to her husband, Adam, who was with her, and he ate it too. At that moment, their eyes were opened, and they suddenly felt shame at their nakedness" (Gen. 3:6–7).

Eve was enticed by the look of the fruit and the mystery of the wisdom it would reveal. Her urge to compromise was stronger than her desire to be obedient. Can you relate? As soon as Eve and Adam believed the lie from Satan, their sin was revealed to them, and they felt shame for their nakedness.

Genesis 3:8—"When the cool evening breezes were blowing, the man and his wife heard the lord God walking about in the garden. They hid from the lord God among the trees." Human nature kicked in. We sinned, so we must hide it or cover it up. It is naive to think we can hide anything from an omnipotent God.

Genesis 3:9–10—Then the Lord God called to Adam, "Where are you?" Adam replies, "I heard you walking in the garden, so I hid. I was afraid because I was naked." Genesis 3:11—"Who told you that you were naked?" the Lord God asked. "Have you eaten from the tree whose fruit I commanded you not to eat?"

Genesis 3:12—The man replied, "*It was the woman you gave me who gave me the fruit, and I ate it.*" Adam passed the buck to Eve, and it sounds like he's blaming God for his choice of women.

Genesis 3:13—Then the lord God asked the woman, "What have you done?" "*The serpent deceived me,*" she replied. "That's why I ate it." Eve passed the buck to the serpent. Adam blamed God and the woman. The woman blamed the serpent, all while the serpent lay basking in the sun, wondering who his next target will be.

Lesson 2

God can't be fooled! He knows everything! He will always love us, but there will be consequences for our disobedience.

When Adam and Eve realized their nakedness, it was God who made clothing from animal skins to clothe them (Gen. 3:21). Do you ever wonder what that moment was like? Did God hand them the clothes, did they instantly appear on their bodies, or did He make the garments and tell them where the dressing room was at? Nevertheless, it had to be the first most humiliating experience to know how much they disappointed the one who created them when their selfish desires won.

This next part is where we realize the full extent of their consequences. God lovingly banished them from the garden and from his presence. He told Adam to cultivate the ground from which he was created. They would live a life apart from God. Their lives would endure hard work, pain, frustration, and, in time, physical death. It was not God's plan! It still is not His plan.

It might be hard to imagine a serpent speaking to anyone, but Satan is the master of disguise. We are foolish if we do not believe it. He does not appear to us in red tights, a long tail, and horns on his head. He is the king of deception; it is his forte. He is known as the father of lies. When we are tempted, it is from Satan. When we are tested, it is from a loving God who wants the best for us. *"Control yourself and be careful!* The devil is your enemy, and he goes around like a roaring lion looking for someone to attack and devour"* (1 Pet. 5:8 [ERV]).

Lions are known for stalking their prey, and when they get close enough to them, they either try to pounce on them or knock them over. They use their powerful claws to maul their prey and crush their heads. The worst part is that a lion has a reputation for playing with their prey before killing them, which can result in a brutal and lengthy cat-and-mouse game. It is not a pretty picture. Satan is clever and dangerous just like the lion.

When thoughts of doubt, fear, temptation, worry, and discouragement enter our minds, it is not from God. Those shoulda, woulda, coulda voices are not helpful.

Anytime we hear a voice contrary to that of our heavenly Father, it is a clear prompting to banish the serpent from the garden of our minds.

Satan will not leave us alone without a fight. He will show up in the most unexpected places. He will remind us of all our mistakes, disappointments, failures, and plant enough fear or worry in our minds to keep us awake feeling restless and without hope. If he cannot get us one way, he will try another way. A lion is relentless. Then just like a sneaky slithering snake, which is often camouflaged or disguised by his surroundings, he'll present a temptation perfectly designed for us. He prods us to cave in to his sinful enticements. When we know it is a temptation, we know it is not from God because God will never tempt us!

God's *voice* always speaks truth! There will not be any confusion. He will give us the courage to own up to sin without blaming others or pointing fingers. God is merciful and gracious. He is always ready to forgive when we humble ourselves and ask Him for it. God knew what He made perfect would become imperfect. He knew sin would enter into the world. God created us as human beings, not robots. He gives us free will to make our own choices. There are researchers now creating artificial intelligence. They are creating robots to think, act, and sound like humans. There is nothing artificial about God's creation. I believe there will be profound consequences for anyone playing God.

What started out as a beautiful day in the garden ended very badly! Adam and Eve succumbed to their own weakness and the serpent's temptation. They could not resist something that looked so good. I know from personal experience that when we act in willful or deliberate violation of God's Word, there is shame, regret, and consequences. No amount of blame, excuses, or justification will make us feel any better.

When we sin, the Bible says to confess it, own up to it. John 1:9, "If we confess our sins he is faithful to forgive us and cleanse us from all unrighteousness." God is omniscient; there's nothing we can hide from Him. There's tremendous freedom in knowing we are forgiven!

In Genesis 3:5–6, Eve was tempted, and she caved in. Scripture gives no indication that she even thought about what she was doing or the consequences. How about you? What would your response be to the serpent's voice? Would you rush in and eat the fruit because it looked so appealing without considering the consequences? There are times that we sin out of our own foolishness. The power of self-satisfaction, deception, or temptation grabs us at our weakest and most vulnerable moments. Sin can be fun; that is why there is so much of it going on in the world. It is short-term pleasure in exchange for eternal consequences. If Satan can keep us fascinated and enticed by sin, he has us right where he wants us. But, eventually, the consequences start to take effect, and it is no longer fun. Sin causes far more hurt and pain in the world than any disease.

King David sought God's testing. "Examine me, God, from head to foot, order your battery of test. Make sure I'm fit inside and out. So, I never lose sight of your love, but keep in step with you, never missing a beat" (Ps. 26:2–2 [The Message]). Asking God to examine our hearts takes courage because truth can be painful. It will expose things in our lives that have been ignored, buried, or denied for a long time. That is the beginning of freedom and the healing process. Once the diagnosis is made, the condition can be treated. Freedom comes when we're no longer trapped by sin and living in a state of shame or guilt.

When Jesus told his disciples that he would have to suffer many terrible things and that he would be rejected and killed, Peter pulled Jesus aside and began to reprimand him for saying such things. Jesus turned around and looked at His disciples, then He reprimanded Peter, "Get behind me, Satan! You are seeing things merely from a human point of view, not from God's."

Lesson 3

Be careful whom we listen to. Satan can be using another person to bring us down.

If the Son of God had to say, "Get behind me, Satan!" how much more should we be saying that when temptation comes our way? Peace and joy are the outcome of a clear conscience and a right relationship with Christ. Do not allow ourselves to get caught up in the blame game or the denial game of life. Take ownership, and we will have freedom!

Father God,

Create in me a clean heart, and renew Your spirit within me. Cast all doubts and fears from me, and bless me with Your presence. Watch over my family and friends. Protect us from becoming complacent in our walk with You. Keep us on guard that we may spot evil and flee from it. Bring to our minds any harm that we have caused another person or any shame we have brought to Your name so we can make it right.

In Jesus's name,

Amen

CHAPTER 3

BUYER BEWARE

The Truth Will Set You Free

We have heard the phrase "Let the buyer beware." It means that the individual buys at one's own risk. Potential buyers are warned by the phrase to do their research and ask pointed questions of the seller. This is often used when purchasing a new home. The seller isn't responsible for the problems that the buyer encounters with the product after the sale.

The three main points above are worth examining from a spiritual perspective. Alexander Hamilton was one of many who used the statement, "If you don't stand for something, you will fall for anything." We go down a very slippery slope when we casually align our beliefs with whatever seems fitting for the day.

1. The individual buys at one's own risk.

To identify precisely how many religions there are in the world today is next to impossible. However, most of those faiths are contained within a handful of major religious groups. There are also about 2 percent of the population that do not believe in any higher power, and that, of course, is another option. Those people are identified as atheist or agnostic. The more options we have, the better chance we'll find something that meets our desires or criteria. If we don't find what we're looking for, create a new one.

For me, the choice is simple because Jesus changed my life! I have also witnessed Him transform the lives of many others. I believe in the Word of God as it is written—Jesus as the only Savior of the world and the Holy Spirit that resides in every born-again believer.

What do you believe?

Fritz Ridenour authors a terrific book about the differences in all major religions. In his book *So What's the Difference*, he writes, "With a veritable smorgasbord of views and opinions now available, it is more important than ever for biblical Christians to be able to recognize and spell out the basic differences between a Christian world-view and the beliefs held by neighbors, coworkers and schoolmates." What we believe in is more important than ever. So, how do we know *what* to believe in and *whom* to worship? Whatever we decide to believe in, it is worth our time to get it right because we are buying at our own risk.

Once we decide what to believe and why, everything in life is easier. All my decisions are filtered by what I believe and whom I believe in. My dad was a godly man, and he was never ashamed to share his testimony. There were times in his life when he would get pushback from people about his faith in Jesus. But whenever he was confronted by someone who didn't believe in the gift of salvation, he would simply say, "If I am wrong, I have nothing to lose, but if you are wrong, you have everything to lose."

There are three ways that Christianity is different from other religions (Chase Culbertson of Newspring Church):

- Every other religion teaches us to earn our way to God. Christianity is the only religion that teaches us that God came to us (Rom. 5:8).

- Other religions have a system of rules to appease a god. Christianity is a relationship with God.

- No other religion has an empty tomb. We're the only people who follow a leader who died and came back to life. Every other major religious leader is dead.

Buyer beware; what we choose to believe will make a difference.

2. Potential buyers are warned to do their research and ask pointed questions.

Before we make a large or costly purchase, my husband always does the research. The old saying is "You get what you pay for." I can tell you from experience that even after doing diligent research on a product, nothing is 100 percent foolproof. If we're willing to give effort to finding the best refrigerator, washing machine, entertainment system, or travel plan, then why wouldn't we do the same for something that is life-changing and eternal?

Here is my perspective: it is easy to put more time and energy into what we can feel, use, see, or enjoy short term. When it comes to our spiritual knowledge, we are a mile wide and an inch deep. Until we begin to do our research and ask pointed questions about what's important eternally, then we will continue to be shallow and uninformed. This following story is about how God transformed the life of an atheist. He did his research and asked pointed questions, but he didn't get the results he was hoping for.

Lee Strobel was an atheist. He was a former legal editor at the *Chicago Tribune*. Strobel was just coming into his own in 1980, fresh off a major investigation of the Ford Pinto controversy, when he decided to apply his journalism skills to a vastly different topic. (In case you are too young to remember, the Ford Pinto, a subcompact car, became infamous in the 1970s for bursting into flames if its gas tank was ruptured in a collision.) As a lawyer, that's the case Lee Strobel was working on.

One evening, Strobel and his family went out for a celebratory dinner. While at the restaurant, their young daughter Alison nearly choked on a gumball. A local nurse was also dining at the same restaurant, and after she saved the child's life, the nurse credited a spiritual prompting she'd been given to eat at that particular restaurant. The encounter lit a spark of faith in Strobel's wife, who soon embraced Christianity and became a regular churchgoer.

This episode and the turn of events in Lee Strobel's life prompted him to research Christianity. He traveled all over the United States to meet with scholars, professors, medical doctors, historians, all to prove that God didn't exist. His complete story can be found in his book *The Case for Christ*.

After probing the evidence for Jesus for nearly two years, Lee became a Christian. All his research backfired! It gave proof that Jesus is the Son of God. He died on the cross, and His body was resurrected from the dead. Lee Strobel is now a *New York Times* best-selling author and the founder of the Lee Strobel Center for Evangelism. Few people do what Lee Strobel had the courage to do. He allowed himself to be proven wrong. He did his research and asked pointed questions. Now, he has impacted the lives of millions of people through his testimony and convictions.

Our faith is nothing to take lightly. We have free choice to believe whatever we want to believe, to worship whomever we want to worship, or to worship no one at all, but we are not free from the consequences of our choices. Joshua 24:15, "But if serving the LORD seems undesirable to you, then choose for yourself this day whom you will serve, whether the gods your ancestors served beyond the Euphrates, or the gods of the Amorites, in whose land you are living. But as for me and my household, we will serve the LORD."

Do our research and then decide what we will believe and whom we will worship. The choice is ours, so are the consequences. Revelation 3:20, "Behold I stand at the door and knock, if anyone hears my voice and opens the door, I will come in and eat with that person, and they with me." God is knocking! God is waiting! Open up the doors of our hearts, and let Him come in. He loves us!

3. The seller isn't responsible for the outcome.

At the end of the day, after doing our research and asking pointed questions, we make our choice and take full responsibility for the outcome.

Our faith and beliefs simply cannot be treated like a buffet dinner where we find lots of options but only take what looks appealing. When we take our last breath, we immediately enter our eternal home. Our bodies can be cremated or buried, but our souls, personality, consciousness are all very much alive in the place we've chosen for eternity. It's all on us! If we've made the choice to accept Jesus Christ as our Lord and Savior and have followed in His ways, we will have an eternal home unmatched by anything ever imagined. We will stand in the presence of a holy God in *His* righteousness, not our own. That will be a *knock-your-socks-off* kind of glorious day!

For those who have chosen any other path, they will stand before a holy God in their *own* righteousness, and heaven will not be an option. When we stand before Christ to give an account of our lives, there will not be room for excuses. God has given us opportunity after opportunity to receive His Son, Jesus, as our personal Savior. Anyone who doesn't accept Christ will be shut out of heaven, just like Adam and Eve were shut out of the Garden of Eden.

Some people find it too confining to only having *one way* to eternal life in heaven. They want there to be many roads that lead to heaven, but that's just not biblical. Jesus said, "But the gateway to life is very narrow the road is difficult, and only a few ever find it" (Matt. 7:15 [NLT]). We can make up our own rules or follow the Word of God, but we cannot do both.

In the introduction to this book, I talked about Alpine skiers and the one percent of athletes who make it as a profession. I guess we could apply the narrow road to them as well. The road is difficult, and only a few ever achieve it. When we want something bad enough, we will be willing to find the narrow road that leads to home.

Here is another way to look at it. Let us say you have a child. You love them so much that you are willing to die in their place. You have provided for them, you have sacrificed for them, you have given them unconditional love and support, and you have corrected them when it was necessary. You have always wanted the best for them. You even set aside a large inheritance for them.

But that child grows up, and they decide they don't want to be your child anymore. They want their freedom to choose another family. They want a family that is more diverse and less restrictive. They want a family on the wide road, so they are willing to walk away from your love and support to get what they think is a better way of life.

As painful as it may be for you, you know the only right thing to do is to let them go. You cannot control them, nor do you want to. The child you brought into the world has turned their back on you. They will forfeit their inheritance. You will still love them, and you would forgive them in a heartbeat. You would take them back with open arms in a minute's notice. But you have let them make their own choice to walk away.

Your child will still reminisce in their mind all the wonderful memories of their childhood. They will always be grateful for all you have done for them. In fact, they will even praise you for that, but they still want to go their own way. They may even say they love you but not enough to stay. This scenario is the same when we choose to pick any other path than Jesus. He will love us always and forever, but we will forfeit the inheritance that He paid for with His life. He will take us back in a heartbeat if we ask Him to. The choice is ours. Is there really any other path worth choosing?

When it comes to buyer beware from a spiritual perspective, be prepared to

- buy into what we believe at our own risk;
- do our research and ask pointed questions; and
- take ownership for our decision in the end.

When we hear of a theology that leaves out Jesus, His death, burial, and resurrection, that is a buyer-beware moment! That is a red flag! The only way to tell the difference between something fake and something authentic is to know the real deal. Jesus is authentic. Do you know Him, I mean really know Him? Does He know you? Have you let Him into your life?

There is no other way to heaven but through the blood of Jesus Christ. Don't be fooled or deceived. If we are uncertain about what or whom to believe, open the Word of God and read the book of John in the New Testament. John was the disciple with the fiery temperament. He also had a special devotion to the Savior. Whenever I'm mentoring people spiritually, I recommend they pray a simple prayer before reading the Bible, asking God to clear their minds and reveal truth to them as they read. Ask God to cleanse our hearts from all unrighteousness, so there are no barriers in our relationship. Find a quiet place to meditate on the Word of God. Ask Him to speak truth into our lives, then listen and watch. He's crazy about us, and He wants us in his family!

Every day, God shows us His handiwork as creation beams with unimaginable beauty, from the intricacies of a flower to the magnificent mountain ranges, to the powerful oceans held within their boundaries by His command. It's in the transformation of a life and the birth of a baby. God is not trying to hide. He's everywhere! He's protecting us in ways we will never know. He loves us and adores us. He will adopt us into his family *when we make him Lord of our lives.* He wants to be our Heavenly Father. Don't miss out!

Karen (Balyeat) Thompson

Heavenly Father,

I come into Your presence with thanksgiving. There are not enough words to express my heartfelt gratitude for all that You have done for me. My sins are forgiven, and my heart is full and complete. I am grateful! My deepest longing is for the salvation of lost souls. Please make a way where there seems to be no way for those who are searching for something on the wide road that leads to nowhere. May their eyes be opened to truth.

Thank You for the peace and hope that come from knowing You. I pray for parents today who are raising a new generation of children. Give young people a spiritual mentor who will point them to You. Raise up strong and "sold out for Jesus" young people who want to make a difference for eternity.

Father, Your word says, "Keep on asking, and you will receive what you ask for. Keep on seeking, and you will find. Keep on knocking, and the door will be opened. For everyone who asks, receives. Everyone who seeks, finds. And to everyone who knocks, the door will be opened" (Matt. 7:7–8 [NLT]).

Father, break our hearts for the things that break Your heart. Do a cleansing in our lives! Prepare us to do Your work.

In the precious name of Jesus,

Amen

CHAPTER 4

THE RACE OF YOUR LIFE

Prepare for the Finish Line

You have all been to a stadium and seen the athletes race. Everyone runs; one wins. Run to win! All good athletes train hard. They do it for a gold medal that tarnishes and fades. You are after one that is gold eternally. I don't know about you, but I'm running hard for the finish line. I am giving it everything I have. No sloppy living for me! I'm staying alert and in top condition. I am not going to get caught napping, telling everyone else all about it and then missing out myself.

—1 Corinthians 9:24–27 (The Message)

This version of scripture has a great visual. I can see the tarnished and faded trophies all lined up. When our sons were young, they played in many different sports. It was fun to watch them participate, and it gave them a chance to see what they enjoyed the most. At the end of the season, it was common for them to bring home a small trophy that represented the sport they had played in. They were inexpensive trophies, but they meant a lot to them at the time. As our sons got older, the trophies lost their meaning. They were just cheap trophies collecting dust that represented a snapshot in their life. For decades, I stored those trophies in a plastic bin in our basement. We had a bin for Jason and a bin for Ben. Finally, with their permission, we got rid of many of them. I am not sure why we hung on to them for so many years, but we did.

Last year, Duane and I watched our granddaughter, Natalie, run cross-country. The event was new to us, and we found the experience to be enlightening. Never had we attended a sporting event where the fans got so actively involved in the race. As spectators, we stood on the sidelines as each runner lined up on the track. Each girl wanted to position herself to have an advantage. They waited anxiously for the sound of the starter pistol. Once the girls heard the crack of the gunfire, they began running, each with her own strategy.

Some runners started slow and kept a steady pace. Others began fast, only to maintain a lead for a fleeting moment as they found themselves running out of breath too early in the race. The crowd yelled out to them, "Stay focused!" "Go!" "You can do it!" "Be patient!" The fans cheered until the runners were out of sight. Then, as if the fans were in the race too, they took off, the parents, grandparents, and friends running as fast as they could to the halfway point of the track. As the runners approached the halfway mark, they could see familiar faces and heard their words of cheer. It was meant to inspire them and to let the runners know the finish line was in sight. The crowd cheered, "Push It!" "You can do it!" "You're almost there!" "Don't give up!" As each runner crossed the finish line with sweat streaming down her face and breathing hard from exhaustion, the cheers continued to ring out, "Good job!" "I'm so proud of you!" "We knew you could do it!" "You never gave up!"

We can all use that kind of fan club in our lives. If we're honest, we'll admit it's so much easier to cheer from the sidelines than it is to be involved in the race. At one of Natalie's events, it had appeared that all the runners had crossed the finish line. People were gathering up their belongings to head home. Then my daughter-in-law pointed out a runner lagging behind. Few people even noticed her. The gal kept running with no indication she was giving up. Then we noticed a man sprinting across the field toward the runner. As he got next to her, he joined her in the race. I asked Rachael, "Is that her coach?" She said, "No, it's her dad."

In that moment, I felt a lump in my throat as I watched the dad run next to his daughter. It's the kind of scene in an inspirational movie. This dad saw his daughter alone on the track but not giving up. He hurried to her side and joined her in the race. They crossed the finished line together. Way to go, Dad! Way to be the pillar for your daughter! I have a feeling the last stretch of that race was much easier with her dad by her side.

We all need accolades! We all need someone to come alongside of us to encourage us or run the race with us when life gets hard. There are people who are running a very difficult race right now. The terrain is steep and rugged. They feel weak, tired, and vulnerable. A low-lying fog is making it difficult to see clearly, or perhaps it's the tears welling up in their eyes. Others are begging for their race to end. The pain is too great to bear. Many are holding out for someone to show them hope—someone to run alongside of them so the race doesn't feel so lonely. We know there's a finish line, and we're all going to cross it. We want to be able to say, "I prepared!" "I endured!" "I persevered!" "I finished well!"

Our heavenly Father is spot-on! He is right there cheering for us. "You can do it! Don't give up! Press on! The finish line is in sight! I'm here for you! I love you, and I will never leave you alone!" We may not see God any more than we see the wind. But when the wind blows, we recognize it as the branches on the trees rustle in the wind. We feel it against our skin and see the subtle movement of our hair and clothes. God wants us to recognize Him as easily as we recognize clouds, sunshine, and the movement of wind. He's not hiding from us! No matter what stage in the race we find ourselves in, do not give up! We have a purpose, and He will come alongside us and help us finish well.

God knows our pain and emotion. He loves us unconditionally. He doesn't care how fast we run or how many fans come to cheer us on. He is enough! He will catch us when we fall and help us get back up. He's in the race with us. He calls us to follow Him. He knows the way to the finish line. A great reward is waiting for us! If we could hear God from the sidelines, I believe he would say, "I know you are tired. Trust me! I know it is hard, but the finish line is in sight. Persevere! I am right here with you!"

Today, our options are many. We can be in as many races as we want. Our kids can be in as many activities as the parents have time to fit into their already busy schedules. There is a race up the corporate ladder—the race to outdo and perform. If we are not careful, life will become more about competing than enjoying the journey. When we give higher importance to our image and appearance rather than being real and authentic, we rob others of knowing the real person. A race with no real importance or payout will leave us feeling exhausted and disappointed.

No one wants to get to the end of their life to find out they've been running a hundred miles an hour in the wrong direction. We can ask ourselves, "What in life is worth chasing after?" "What will make the biggest impact?" "What will be my legacy?" As I read the book of Ecclesiastes, I am reminded of all the things we put value on that have no meaning or lasting value. At the end of the book of Ecclesiastes 12:13, King Solomon writes, "Here now is my final conclusion: Fear God and obey his commands ..." That is what matters.

Hebrews 12:1b, "So let us run with perseverance the race marked out for us." This verse tells us that we aren't made for every race but only those that have been marked out for us. I learned this lesson a long time ago. While I was still working and raising a family, I did volunteer work for Child Protective Services, I was a youth group leader at our church, and I served on numerous boards and committees. This went on for years. Then God revealed this to me: "Find out what I want you to do, and say no to the rest."

After that revelation, it became a lot easier for me to make decisions about how I would spend my time. The Bible says that God gives everyone a gift, but not everyone has all the gifts. Once we discover our God-given gifts, we're able to focus on God's purpose for our lives. It simplifies the race.

2 Timothy 4:7, "I have fought the good fight, I have finished the race, I have kept the faith." Sloppy living is our *slippery slope*. Running without a purpose is futile. Tombstones are marked by two dates and a dash. What will others say about your legacy and the time you spent between birth and death? We can be sure of this: when God is in the spaces of our lives, we'll never have to look back with regret. When we allow God to chart our

course, we'll finish well! My prayer is that we will join the marathon and keep pace with our loving heavenly Father.

We are all on a path going somewhere. Are you in the race or standing on the sidelines? Do you know where you're headed, or are you on some random course that has no clear direction? Jesus says, "Follow me …" Christianity is not complicated! When we come to the finish line in our lives, we want to be sure we've followed Him into eternity. Will you accept Him today as your Lord and Savior by praying this simple prayer? It doesn't matter how we start the race, but it matters how we finish.

Father God,

I come to You with a humble and repentant heart. I confess that I am a sinner in need of a Savior. I believe Your Son, Jesus, is my only hope. I believe Jesus died on the cross for my sins. I believe Jesus spent three days in a tomb until He was resurrected by Your power—the same power that created the universe and all creation. It's the same power of His resurrection that assures me of eternal life in heaven.

Your Word says that once I accept You as my Lord and Savior, I will become Your child and I will spend eternity with You. Today, I choose to follow You!

In Jesus's name,

Amen

CHAPTER 5

WHAT ARE YOU SO AFRAID OF?

In Your Weakness, He Is Strong

Do not be afraid, for I am with you. Do not
be discouraged, for I am your God. I will
strengthened you and help you. I will hold
you up with my victorious right hand.
—Isaiah 41:10 (NLT)

If you skim over this verse without letting it sink in, that
will be a big mistake! Say it again: Do not be afraid! Do
not be discouraged! I will help you!

From our earliest days, we experience fear. Fear of
the dark. Fear of being alone. Fear of missing out. Fear
of noises, nightmares, spiders, and storms. My dad had
the innate ability to make really scary noises. As a little
girl, I remember turning the corner from our living

room to head down the hallway to my bedroom. As I went around the corner, I saw my dad on his hands and knees crawling toward me, making scary noises. Once he realized how much he had scared me, he felt bad.

"Fear is a powerful emotion. At its best, it can protect us from danger and motivate us to do the right thing. But at its worst, fear can hold us back from reaching our full potential" (Stephanie Larratt, *Today*).

Fear is something we learn about ourselves. It's not the same for everyone. When our boys were young, we took them to Disney World. Ben, our youngest, was about eight years old at the time. Duane and I thought it would be fun for our family to ride the Big Thunder Mountain Railroad. We told the boys, "This will be fun!" Disney World can be crazy busy, so waiting in a lengthy line is just part of the experience. When it was finally our turn, we each stepped into our seats and pulled the crossbar down over our laps to keep us safe and secure. When all the other passengers were strapped in, the train began slowly chugging along, taking us through a haunted gold mine in roller-coaster style. The train gained speed with each twist and turn. It did not take long to notice the fear on Ben's face. He held on tight to the grip bar and snuggled up close to his dad. I thought he was going to wriggle right out of his seat. It was painful to watch!

When the train stopped, it was clear that this ride was anything but fun for Ben. He was stuck on the Big Thunder Mountain train ride that he didn't like, and he couldn't get off. Have you ever felt like that? Can you relate? When we're afraid, we cower down. We feel trapped, unprotected, insecure, and out of control.

Some encounters have such an impact on us that they live in the archives of our memory. They quickly come to surface when we see or hear something that reminds us of that anxious encounter. Our fear may not be of scary noises or roller-coaster rides; but whatever it is, it can be paralyzing. What keeps you awake at night? What do you think about that leaves you feeling anxious or uncomfortable? Pinpointing our fears is the first step in overcoming them. Chances are, we have more than one fear; I know I do. Fear can lead to anxiety, and anxiety can lead to fear.

What I have learned about fear is that there are many different degrees. There are the fears that we accumulate overtime—for example,

- fear of failure and disappointment;
- fear that those you love will reject the plan of salvation;

- fear of losing everything you've worked hard for;
- fear of a debilitating illness;
- fear of letting go of control; and
- fear of being found out from what you've been desperately trying to hide.

Then there are reactive fears:

- A hurricane is headed your way.
- You have come upon a bad car accident.
- There is a significant drop in the stock market.
- There is an alert that you need a second health screening.
- Your child is late coming home.

There are fears that have to be overcome in a minute's notice, or someone will die:

- You pull a victim from a burning car.
- You run through the woods late at night to rescue a child.
- Your spouse has a heart attack, and you need to act now!

It's a wonderful thing when we come to the point where we face our most dreaded fears and replace them with faith.

There are many people in history who have shown us what it looks like to move forward despite their fear. Alan B. Shepherd was the first American astronaut to be hurled into orbit in a rocket. The disciple Simon Peter stepped out of the boat in the middle of the sea to walk on water toward Jesus. Jessica Watson, the sixteen-year-old from Sydney, Australia, attempted to sail solo and unassisted around the world. Her story is inspiring. Her parents were the ones that let her live her dream despite their fears. They knew she would face unimaginable challenges out in the middle of the ocean.

Corrie Ten Boom is a woman I deeply admire. She was an unassuming woman living in Holland during the Nazi occupation. Ten Boom was well into her forties when the Germans invaded the Netherlands during World War II. She and her family joined others in sheltering and guiding Jews and other refugees to safety. It's recorded that she and her family may have saved over eight hundred Jews. When Corrie and her family made the decision to hide the Jews from the Germans, they knew their own lives were at risk. They chose courage over fear. One of her greatest quotes is "The measure of a life, after all, is not its duration but its donation." I am so thankful for those who have gone before us with selfless courage.

Every day and in every country, people face tremendous fear. Their fears are real! It is not an imagination of what can happen; they are living with warranted fear. Some mothers watch their children die from starvation or illness and there is no remedy. People in high-crime areas put metal bars over their windows to deter burglars. The COVID pandemic had millions of people hunkered down in their homes for months, too afraid to go out into public places. Some fear is warranted. But I believe most fear comes from *our invited thoughts* that we have allowed to enter our minds, and when we do, the fear stays way too long. We talk about it. We dwell on it, and then it becomes attached to our lives and begins to impact our decisions and health.

This story is about how I let reactive fear control me. Years ago, Duane and I went to Washington State to visit his brother, Bill, and family. It would be our first trip to the Evergreen State. Once we arrived, Bill and his wife, Shari, explained how they wanted to take us on a camping excursion in the Hoh Rain Forest. It is located about four hours northwest of Seattle, Washington. So it would be a little jaunt to get there.

Bill and Shari would be using their small pop-up camper to sleep in. Duane and I and our one-and-a-half-year-old son would be using their bottomless tent to sleep in. This did not sound like a dream vacation to me, but we agreed to the plan. Don't get me wrong; I love the outdoors, but I would much rather spend my sleeping hours in a king-size bed in a safe, comfortable, and clean motel.

Once we entered the Hoh Rain Forest, we started our gradual ascent to the campsite. We climbed several miles up a long, winding road. The large Sitka spruce and western red cedars were covered with big clumps of hanging moss. It was anything but appealing to me. The backdrop of the overcast sky gave it a very eerie look. It wasn't at all what I was hoping for. Duane tried being more optimistic; it was his brother taking us there.

Once we reached our secluded campsite, we found it nestled next to a lovely stream surrounded by rocks and boulders. We had arrived just before dusk, giving us little time to set up our tent for the evening. At bedtime, Duane and I snuggled into our cozy sleeping bags, making sure Jason was covered and secure in his playpen, which was just a couple of feet from us. I pulled the sleeping bag over my head as a precaution for any little critter that might find our place to be inviting. It was the least I could do.

The only sounds we could hear that night were a concert of humming, chirping, and bullfrogs. I tried to resist letting my mind wander too far between the night noises, the eerie look of the moss on the trees, and our open tent. I was physically tired but could not sleep. As we settled in, Duane was so quiet, I couldn't tell if he was sleeping or, like me, afraid to move. Suddenly, I felt something small and fast run across my covered face. I did not know what it was, but it had just confirmed my fear. Thank God I had pulled that sleeping bag over my head! Hours later, still wide awake and anxious, I heard the thumping sound of something *big* outside our tent. Was it a bear? We were in bear country! I nudged Duane to see if he was awake. Whatever it was, I didn't want to experience it alone. He said, "I hear it, be quiet!" My heart was pounding so hard, it's a wonder it didn't jump out of my skin. We waited until the sound passed by, hoping our baby boy wouldn't wake up crying. Fear had crept into our tent, and my body was in knots. I was glad Duane was awake and heard the heavy steps too; otherwise, I might have been accused of having a nightmare.

If we had not been afraid, we might have foolishly poked our heads out of the opening of the tent to see what was out there. Instead, fear kept our bodies quiet and still. I'd like to say we had a healthy dose of fear that night, but was it? I like to tell this story occasionally because it left such a visual impact on me. The sights, sounds, noises, unfamiliar territory were a sure recipe for a night to remember.

Fear is a natural response to many things, but when it controls us, it can become the *slipperiest slope we*'ll ever go down. It prompts exaggeration. That night in the forest, my fear started on the drive to the campsite. It was gradual. Nothing was scary except my imagination. I had nothing to fear but fear itself. Granted we encountered critters, and maybe even a big one, but we're still here to talk about it. We will never know what it was.

Fear has a way of lingering. My father died at the age of sixty-five from an inoperable malignant brain tumor. I breathed a sigh of relief when each of my siblings and I passed the age of sixty-five in good health. The thought of one of us having a brain tumor lingered in the back of my mind for years. It didn't consume me, but I thought about it more than I would like to admit. Once we commit to listening to the voice of fear, it can drain us and take our minds to very dark places.

I have heard that "fear not" is recorded in the Bible 365 times. There is a verse for every day of the year. Our heavenly Father knows that fear is something we will have to deal with all of our lives. He is telling us that no matter what we go through in life, He will be there for us and help us to get through it. When there's that many verses about one topic in the Bible, it is worth memorizing one of them.

The *slippery slope* of fear can be like quicksand; it can take us down and draw us in with uncontrolled force. We feel trapped with no escape route. The Bible says, "Call on me when you are in trouble, and I will rescue you, and you shall glorify me" (Ps. 50:15 [NLT]). Scripture isn't just a nice book to read. It is the inspired Word of God, the maker of heaven and earth. There's no philosopher, theologian, astronomer, teacher, politician, professor, or author who can give you more wisdom and truth than the inspired Word of God. God cannot be compared to anyone! He stands alone! When God says, "Call on Me," that's exactly what He means.

Jesus is no stranger to fear. He can totally relate.

Before He went to the cross to be crucified, He prayed, "Father, if you are willing, please take this cup of suffering from me. Yet I want your will to be done, not mine. Then an angel from heaven appeared and strengthen him. He prayed more fervently, and he was in such agony of spirit that his sweat fell to the ground like drops of blood" (Luke 22:42–44 [NLT]).

Jesus prayed that prayer three times. He knew that all the sin and sickness of the world would come upon Him on the cross. He knew His Father would turn away from Him and demons would torment Him. We have a Savior who understands our fears, and He wants us to trust Him. God is our only hope! He understands!

God turned his back on His Son during His greatest time of suffering because we needed a Savior! Without Jesus's death and resurrection, there would be no hope of salvation or eternal life. Christ's suffering was necessary for our redemption. Fear didn't keep Jesus from the cross; obedience and faith held Him there. His love for you and me held him there. He did it all for us despite the fear and agony that He experienced.

Fear is one of Satan's greatest weapons. If he can make us fearful, he has diminished our faith. It will rob our lives of happiness and joy. It will keep us awake at night and leave us feeling anxious. Every time the slippery slope of fear comes upon us, remind God that we need His victorious right hand to lift us up. Talk to Him. Rely on Him. God wants our faith and trust to be in Him. If you are at a place where fear is sucking the life out of you, then seek out a friend, a pastor, or counselor. Ask a trustworthy person to pray with you.

Nothing is impossible for God! We can overcome fear when we put our faith in Him. God wants us to live a life free from fear.

Heavenly Father,

You are the Alpha and Omega, the beginning, and the end. You know all things past, present, and future, and yet You say, "Fear not!" God, it's all about trusting in You! Forgive me for worrying about things that I should be giving to You because You are the burden carrier.

Father, when world events get me in a frenzy, remind me to trust You. When I begin to worry about my grandchildren and the battles and temptations they face from the internet and social media, remind me to trust in You. When my daughter-in-law goes in for her cancer screening, remind me to trust in You. When Duane and I wonder about our future and health concerns, remind us to trust in You. You are the God of Angel Armies! We call upon You today. Help us put all of our fears into Your hands and leave them there.

In Jesus's name,

Amen

CHAPTER 6

LIGHTEN UP!

Live Unashamed

I am the light of the world. If you follow me,
you will not have to walk in darkness, because
you have the light that leads to life.
—John 8:12 (NLT)

Jesus is giving us an option. He identifies himself as the Light. Then He says, "If you follow me, you won't have to walk in darkness." We won't be stumbling around. It's a choice. It's always a choice. I have a wild imagination, so I am not a fan of being in the dark too long. I can scare myself just by thinking about creepy things. I was touring the inside of Mammoth Cave when the tour guide turned his lamp off to prove a point. I did not know that darkness could feel so cold, void, and empty.

I could not see my own hand when it was in front of my face. It was total blackness. The only sound you could hear was that of slow dripping water. We needed the lamp turned on to find our way out and to avoid hitting our heads on low mineral formations. The floor of the cavern was slippery in places, so we stood perfectly still until the light was turned back on. The light was needed for guidance and protection. Jesus is that light for our everyday lives if we choose to follow Him.

When I was a little girl going to children's church, we would sing "This Little Light of Mine." As a six-year-old, I had no idea what the song really meant. But I sang the catchy tune because all the other kids were singing it too. I knew the light was a good thing and that Satan was bad, and he would try to blow out my candlelight and that wasn't an option. That was all I needed to know.

Fast forward seven years, and I'm living in the American bandstand, rock and roll era. Best time ever! The rock group The Doors came out with a hit song, "Light My Fire." The lyrics "come on baby light my fire" had a whole different meaning than the one I sang about in children's church. It was a different kind of light. During my teenage years, Jesus took a back seat in my life. I didn't think too much about Him unless

I needed to ask for forgiveness. I had gone to church enough to know that sin was bad, and I knew when I was doing something I should not be doing. So I would talk to God often at bedtime just to make sure if I died during the night, I would still go to heaven. It is funny how we think as children, but some adults still live that way. They will go and party all night, then ask for forgiveness. I doubt that lack of sincerity goes far, but God knows our hearts.

I made it through school on a wing and a prayer. My parents had a few more gray hairs. I was the youngest of three children, so by the time I was done with high school, they were ready to be empty nesters.

It was just seven months after my high school graduation that I moved to Colorado Springs, Colorado, and married Duane. My parents found a sense of relief knowing that I was marrying a pretty stable guy who was in the army. Three years later, I became pregnant with our first son. We did a lot of growing up in our first three years of marriage. Duane's father was killed in a tragic car accident six weeks after we were married. That will make you grow up fast! Duane and I also survived serious injury from a bad car accident. In a separate incident, Duane broke his ankle and was in a cast for six weeks. Those events and the sheer adjustments to living in another state and being newly married were enough to grow us up.

After Duane was discharged from the army, we moved back to Indiana to be close to family. We wanted to find jobs, buy a home, and start a family. My wonderful parents let us live with them for six months so we could save enough money for a down payment on our first home. It worked out well. Shortly after we moved into our own place, I got pregnant with our first child. We were so excited! I tell you this story because my walk with Jesus has been a journey. It was during my pregnancy that I became very thoughtful about what it was going to mean to be a mother. I began to think about the kind of mom I wanted to be. I was a decent person, but I was not a Christian. I knew enough about what it meant to be saved, so I knew I was living outside the will of God. I wanted that to change.

I had a Bible that I had not opened for years; it was one my parents had bought me. I knew that the Bible was the inspired Word of God. I knew God loved me no matter what, but my life was missing something. There was a void in my life. On a sweltering summer August afternoon, while I was six months pregnant, I put my hand on top of my dusty Bible and began to pray. I asked God to forgive me for my sins, and I invited Him into my life. It was a choice I made to follow the light of Jesus.

My eyes were opened, and I could see all the barriers that I had put up to keep God out of my life. If you want truth, God will show it to you. A whole new world opened for me. The switch was turned on, and everything became clearer. Jesus had dispelled the darkness. From my early years at children's church to my rebellious teenage years, darkness had gradually moved into my life. Did you know that if we live in darkness long enough, our eyes will adjust to it? We won't even realize what we're missing. It is like adjusting a dimmer switch to our lives until we can barely tell the light is on. Darkness is profound! If our homes were void of windows and we never turned a light on, we would never see how dirty our houses are. The same is true for our hearts. God is the only one who can shine light into our lives. My life went full circle from the little girl who was introduced to Jesus but did not understand it all to the teenager who rebelled, to the mother-to-be who wanted to live her best life as a new mom. Surrendering to Jesus was the best decision I ever made.

Jesus understands what it feels like to have our light threatened. He was popular. He was well known. He was loved by those who knew Him and hated by those who didn't understand Him or found Him to be a threat. When King Herod heard about the birth of the Messiah, he ordered all the children in Bethlehem two years and younger to be killed. He was hoping that Jesus would be among the many children who were killed, but God had a different plan. Herod did not want any competition. He didn't want anyone worshipping the newborn king. God protected Jesus despite Herod's evil attempt to have Him killed. Herod wanted to snuff out the light of the living Savior.

In Matthew 5:14–16 (NLT), Jesus told his disciples, "You are the light of the world, like a city on a hilltop that cannot be hidden. No one lights a lamp, and then puts it under a basket. Instead, a lamp is placed on a stand, where it gives light to everyone living in the house. In the same way, let your virtuous deeds shine out for all to see, so that everyone will praise our heavenly Father." Jesus is telling us today to behave in a manner that others will see the light of Christ in our lives. We are not to do good deeds so others can pat us on the back and acknowledge our good works. We do charitable deeds to honor our God.

God never calls us to shine the light on ourselves. It would backfire! It would reveal our inadequacies, weaknesses, and flaws. The light is all about sharing what God has done for us. If your faith is at a place where you have a story to tell, be prepared to share it when God opens a door for you. Most of us would not hesitate to jump in to help someone during a tragedy. But when it comes to talking about the only one who can save a soul from death and destruction, the devil has us tongue tied, and that's just the way he likes it. We will never be able to save anyone, but we can sure point them to the one who can.

As Jesus was speaking to a crowd, He said, "If any of you wants to be my follower, you must turn from your selfish ways, take up your cross and follow me. If you try to hang on to your life, you will lose it. But if you give up your life for my sake, you will save it. And what do you benefit if you gain the whole world, but are yourself lost or destroyed? If anyone is ashamed of my message, the Son of Man will be ashamed of that person when he returns in His glory and in the glory of the Father and the Holy Angels" (Luke 9:23–26 [NLT]).

Every slippery slope has a consequence. And being too proud, too insecure, too fearful to talk about Jesus falls right into the hands of what Satan likes. We need to be a threat to Satan! "For God has not given us a spirit of fear and timidity, but of power, love and self discipline" (2 Tim. 1:7 [NLT]). He calls us to be the light of the world.

Our pastor tells a story about playing basketball in his senior year of high school. He admits he wasn't one of the best players despite his athletic physique. During one of his games, he continued to be wide open from three-point range. He took several missed shots before being pulled out of the game by his coach. When the coach scolded him for taking the missed shots, he said, "But I was wide open!" The coach responded, "There's a reason you were wide open—you aren't a threat!" That was a humbling experience for the player. But what about you—are you a threat to Satan, or does he not have to worry about you?

Our world is a very dark place, and people need hope! God offers hope! We never need to apologize, explain away, or back down from our call to honor and glorify Him. While I was at a work conference, they divided all the attendees into small groups of ten during a breakout session. I was sitting with people I had never met before. After several minutes of conversation, a lady in the group looked at me and asked me about my life's priorities. I am sure I looked surprised because I was. It could have been an intimating question, but, without hesitation, I said, "God is first in my life, then my husband, and then my family." I don't remember what I said after that, but I remember feeling anxious by the question. But she looked at me with a smile and said, "Now I understand." I'm not always that quick on my feet, but I thank God for giving me those words. God was glorified that day.

It is not easy to live a consistent life because life is hard! My light has been dimmed many times as I've felt consumed by the cares of the world. That is why my goal for each day is to begin with prayer and spend at least a few minutes in either the Bible or a good devotional book. I need the words of wisdom found in scripture. Those few minutes help to jump-start my day.

I come away knowing that I have off-loaded all my concerns to God. He is the burden bearer. Scripture says in 1 Peter 5:7, "Give all your worries and cares to God, for he cares about you." When we give God our cares, it shows Him that we trust Him to handle them.

He is not just the one who carries our burdens, but He is our heavenly Father, and He wants to encourage us, protect us, and guide us. When we spend time with

Him, He will prepare us to represent Him well. A few years ago, I was visiting an aunt of mine. As we were talking about church and what we believed, she excused herself from the room to go get her Bible. When she came back, she had a nice white box in her hand. She carefully opened it up, and inside was a beautiful white Bible. It was her prized possession. As I left that evening, it struck me that all God's words of wisdom were locked up inside that white box. All the Bibles and devotional books in the world won't make us stronger unless we read them.

How would you feel if your child went to school for thirteen years and still didn't know how to read or do simple math because he or she never opened a book? If we want to become good at something, we must put in the effort. We understand that from a secular point of view, but the same is true for our faith.

Jesus did not come into the world to condemn the world but to save the world (John 3:17). We are not to condemn the world either. Jesus says, "Let your light so shine before men, that they may see your good works, and glorify your Father in heaven" (Matt. 5:16 [KJV]). I have found that the more comfortable I am with my faith the easier it is to share it. When we fully grasp the height and depth of God's love for us, we'll want to tell everyone. God not only sent his Son Jesus to die for our sins but also invites us into His family. "He has enabled you to share in the inheritance that belongs to his people, who live in the light" (Col. 1:12 [NLT]). This inheritance includes salvation, strength, hope, peace, comfort, providence, fellowship, and so much more. That news is too wonderful not to share. Be bold, be brave, and live unashamed for the glory of God because, in the end, nothing else will matter. I am no longer a little girl singing "This Little Light of Mine" but a woman of faith who wants to let her light shine for the glory of God.

Every day is not easy, but it's always worth it.

Father God,

You are the light of the world. You shine into the darkness not only to expose sin and shame but also to guide us into Your presence. Father, do a cleansing in my life so that I will be prepared to share my faith as You give me opportunities. It is with a grateful heart that I say thank You! Thank You for being the kind of father who knows everything about me and loves me unconditionally. You see every flaw and every good intention that never gets completed. You hear my heart cry out to You for strength and wisdom. God, sometimes it is simply hard to be the light when there is so much darkness in the world. Please give every believer the boldness to trust You more. Give us hearts that love well. And for those who are still living in darkness, God, speak to their hearts and open their eyes to truth.

In Jesus's name,

Amen

CHAPTER 7

DUST OFF YOUR LENSES

Live a Focused Life

We don't yet see things clearly. We're squinting in
a fog, peering through a mist. But it won't be long
before the weather clears and the sun shines bright.
We will see it all then, see it all as clearly as God
sees us, knowing him directly just as he knows us!
—1 Corinthians 13:12 (The Message)

But for right now, until that completeness, we have
three things to do to lead us toward consummation:
trust steadily in God,
hope unswervingly,
love extravagantly.
And the best of the three is love.
—1 Corinthians 13:13 (The Message)

In this scripture, the apostle Paul is writing to the church of Corinth. He had an honest discussion with them about the issues that impacted people in the first century. Paul provided an important model for how the church should handle the problems of sin in their midst.

He gave them a spiritual lens to look through. He told the church in 1 Corinthians 13:13 that, until they were complete or made perfect in Christ, they had three things to do. It's the same for you and me.

Trust steadily in God!

Hope unswervingly!

Love extravagantly!

We can find ourselves on a very *slippery slope* when our lives get out of focus, when we forget what is important and become consumed in the immediate, when spending time with God has dropped off our radar, when we cannot recall the last time we talked to Him. Our calendars dictate our coming and going. Each day is a mirror reflection of yesterday and a projection of what tomorrow will be. We are squinting in the fog, peering through the mist because our lives have gotten out of focus. But because of God's grace, it won't be long until we see clearly. So clean your lenses and get ready!

Scripture reminds us of Satan's schemes. "Satan, who is the god of this world, has blinded the minds of those who do not believe. They are unable to see the glorious light of the Good News. They do not understand the message about the glory of Christ, who is the exact likeness of God" (2 Cor. 4:4 [NLT]).

How about you? Can you see clearly, or do your lenses need an upgrade? Over the years, my eyesight has changed. Without glasses or contact lenses, everything is a blur. I cannot function without them. I rely on them every minute of my waking hours. When I roll out of bed in the morning, my eyes are out of focus, so I reach for my glasses as a quick fix. But, when I'm negligent with my time with God, my heart develops the "lazy eye syndrome," becoming out of focus. I call it "the distraction dilemma" or "the notion of good intention."

The distraction dilemma has become our norm: phone calls, emails, text messages, notifications, social media, and other people. When Jesus needed to prepare a talk or pray, He found a solitary place. He had one agenda, and that was to find a quiet place where He could hear from His Father. If Jesus, the Son of God, needed a quiet time, how much more do we need it?

Do not miss it! Jesus found a quiet place so He could hear from His Father. It takes a lot of coffee, self-talk, and discipline for me to stay alert and mentally focused. The notion of good intention is "I'll do it tomorrow." This is especially true in our retirement years because we always have tomorrow. We don't mean to let good intentions fall through the cracks of our lives, but they easily do. Most of the time, when we find our spiritual lives out of focus, we can look back and see that either distractions won out or our good intentions were put on the shelf for a later time. Until our spiritual vision is 20/20, the apostle Paul says there are three things we can do.

Trust Steadily!

Trust can be hard! If we were raised in a home that was critical and harsh, we might think that God is the same way. If our parents were detached and too busy for us, we might picture God that way too. If we've been hurt by people who were supposed to protect us, we might hesitate to put our wholehearted trust in God. We are looking through a clouded lens. Attaching less than perfect attributes to God is as far from the truth as we can get. God is perfect; people are not!

It is a sad day when our earthly examples fail us, and we attach those same characteristics to our heavenly Father. Please do not allow those who have disappointed you to become your perception of God. No one can compare to our Lord and Savior! All of us have been disappointed. We must keep our eyes on the Perfect One. He is trustworthy!

Scripture says, "Trust in the Lord with all your heart; do not depend on your own understanding. Seek his will in all you do, and he will direct your paths" (Prov. 3:5 [The Living Bible]. It starts with trust and ends with God directing our path. If you have never put your trust in God, today is a perfect day to start.

Hope Unswervingly!

Do not give up on hope. "The Lord your God is with you, the Mighty Warrior who saves. He will take great delight in you, in his love he will no longer rebuke you, but will rejoice over you with singing" (Zeph. 3:17). Hold on to hope! Our God is for us not against us! Let these names of God give us hope.

God is also known as the following:

Adonai	Lord or Master
El Olan	the Everlasting God
El Shaddai	All Sufficient One
Jehovah Jireh	the Lord will Provide
Jehovah Rapha	the Lord that Heals
Jehovah Raah	the Lord my Shepherd
Jehovah Shalom	the Lord is Peace

We all need unswerving hope—hope that is not based on human knowledge but on the Word of God. Have you ever looked up in the night sky and been amazed by the thousands and thousands of stars? Scripture asks, "Who created all the stars? He brings them out like an army one after the other, calling each by its name. Because of his great power and incomparable strength, not a single one is missing" (Isa. 40:26 [NLT]).

My friend, if God knows the name of every star and not one goes missing, you can be sure of this: He knows your name, and you will never be out of his sight. Hope is not dreaming. Hope is confidence that God will complete everything He has promised in His Word. He is faithful! Put your hope in Him today.

Love Extravagantly!

The most recognized verse in the Bible is found in John 3:16–17. "For this is how God loved the world: He gave his one and only Son, so that everyone who believes in him will not perish but have eternal life. God sent his son into the world not to judge the world, but to save the world through him."

God's love is perfect and unchanging. When our lives get out of focus and we grow distant from Him, He is still there with 20/20 vision, waiting on us to come back. His love is our best example of how to love others. He loved us before we became his followers; while our lives were still drenched in sin, He loved us. He always will! We never need to clean up our act before coming to God. That work will be done by God in the workshop of our lives. His invitation for us is to "come as you are!" No filters! Just run to Jesus, and He will receive you with open arms.

Jesus showed his unwavering love by being engaged. He had a mission, and it always included people. He took quality time with them. He was never rushed or in a hurry. He led his team of disciples with authority while showing compassion. He spent time with his heavenly Father every day. He also made it clear to his disciples that he needed a break from them so he could rest and spend time alone with His Father.

If Jesus, the Son of God, thought it was important to pray, then how much more should we feel the importance in our own lives? He taught His followers how to pray. We call it the Lord's Prayer. He was focused in His prayer life.

F. Fatherly focused: "Our Father which art in heaven, Hallowed be thine Name."

O. Obedient: "Thy Kingdom come, thy will be done in earth as it is in heaven."

C. Confidence and confession: "Give us this day our daily bread. And forgive us our trespasses, as we forgive those who trespass against us."

U. Unblemished: "And lead us not into temptation but deliver us from evil."

S. Sovereign: "For thine is the kingdom the power and the glory forever and ever." Amen.

God desires that our prayers acknowledge his sovereignty. We pray with a humble heart asking for His will to be done, not our will. We approach his throne with confidence knowing He will provide all our needs and forgive all our sins as we acknowledge them before Him. It is His power and glory that make all things possible. Our spiritual vision will become 20/20 as we look through His eyes of wisdom and grace.

What is it that blurs your spiritual vision? Is it a wrong perception of who God is? Have you been let down by Christians? Has the Church disappointed you? Do you find the Bible too complicated? Are you just content going with the flow and hoping everything works out for you in the end? What is it that keeps you from being sold out for Jesus Christ?

Whenever I am coaching someone or mentoring them spiritually, I make it very clear to them that their focus needs to be on Jesus. I can promise them that I will spend quality time with God to prepare and that I will be trustworthy, but I am far from perfect. It is important for us to know who we are and what we are not. God is perfect; we are not! I have been disappointed too; who hasn't been? So I understand what it feels like to be let down. But I am equally sure that I have been the one to disappoint. We need to be quick to forgive and show ample grace. Because what we give to others today may be just what we need tomorrow from them.

I encourage us to keep our eyes on Jesus. If our lenses are blurred for whatever reason, ask God to give us spiritual insight. If we have questions about the Bible, ask for help in understanding. When we stand before our Holy God, there will be no excuses. We won't be able to say, "I didn't go to church because Billy hurt my feelings," "I didn't read the Bible because it was too hard to understand," or "I didn't give financially because, dog-gone it, I worked too hard for my money to give it away." When we are standing face-to-face with a Holy God, all excuses will go up in smoke. Be prepared to give an account of our lives, not someone else's. We can stand with confidence before our Heavenly Father when we trust steadily, hope unswervingly, and love extravagantly for Jesus's sake.

Father God,

Thank You for being our greatest example. Thank You for giving us hope! Thank You for loving us enough to clear our clouded vision. Help us open Your Word so that we can see clearly all that You desire for us this side of eternity.

Your love is extravagant! You are worthy of our worship and adoration! Stop us, Lord, from allowing the distractions of this world to be an excuse for complacency. Turn our focus off of things, other people, our selfish desires and on to what matters most to You. Help us to discern what is temporal and what is eternal.

Forgive us for wasting time and drifting off course. You are the great Shepherd. We need You to come after us and bring us back so our lives are in focus with Your will and Your ways. Help us to hear Your voice and listen as You guide us with Your perfect vision. Help our number-one priority be to honor and obey You.

In the mighty name of Jesus,

Amen

CHAPTER 8

WHERE'S GOD IN ALL OF THIS?

He Will Never Leave You

Nothing in all creation is hidden from God's sight.
Everything is uncovered and laid bare before the
eyes of him to whom we must give an account.
—Hebrews 4:13 (NIV)

I had a conversation with my granddaughter, Haley, about how Secret Service agents protect our government officials and their families. I mentioned that there wasn't a place that President Obama's girls could go without an agent being close by. The agents may stand outside a room or sit in a car, but they always knew where the girls were at and whom they were with.

I got the feeling that Haley thought that kind of hovering was an invasion of privacy. I totally understand her point of view. As much as the Secret Service wants to allow freedom, they are responsible for the protection and well-being of those they are assigned to.

I could not help but draw the analogy between God and the Secret Service. The God of the Bible is omniscient.

There is not a secret to be had. He knows our thoughts, He sees through walls, He sees our actions, and He knows our motives behind everything we do. That should be enough to keep us on our toes. Nothing is hidden from His sight. There's no being incognito around God. He will recognize us anywhere. He is our Dad!

I remember meeting our son, Ben, at the O'Hare International Airport in Chicago. He was traveling home from Portland, Oregon. His dad and I looked down the corridor of the airport, and we spotted our son. His 6'3" frame, ginger hair, and stride were the identifying markers. He was our son, and we would recognize him anywhere. We are God's children, and He knows our name. He will recognize us anywhere.

The Hebrew word for "shield" is *Magen* (ma-GAIN). God is my shield and my protector. We may not see or know all that God protects us from, but He does protect us. Our God is the God of Angel Armies. "He will command his angels concerning you to guard you in all your ways" (Ps. 91:11 [NIV]).

In Billy Graham's book *Angels—Ringing Assurance That We Are Not Alone,* he says, "I do not believe in angels because I have ever seen one—because I haven't. I believe in angels because the Bible says there are angels; and I believe the Bible to be the true Word of God." I believe that too!

When our president leaves the White House, he expects Secret Service to have done their due diligence to provide him and his family safety to the best of their ability. As skilled, disciplined, and trained as they might be, they will never compare to the protection that God and His heavenly host give us 24/7.

We can lose sight of God's protection, but He never loses sight of us. We are not alone! There are countless examples in the Bible where bad things happened to good people. Does it mean that God fell asleep like Jesus did in the fishing boat when the storm was raging? No! He calmed the storm.

Did God wright the wrong script when He said He was going to protect us? Our stories aren't finished. Did God forget about David when his brothers threw him into a pit to die? No! David was captured and made a king. Did God take a vacation when Job lived through tragedy upon tragedy? No! God restored him. Did God forsake His own Son Jesus on the cross? If God had intervened, you and I would not have a Savior or path to eternal life.

When we look at tragedies without looking at the purpose, we miss the meaning. Let's look at Jonah's life.

Do you remember Jonah and the whale? True story! Jonah was swallowed up by a massive fish when he tried to run from God. Running will get you nowhere! God knows where we are all the time. You see, God gave Jonah an assignment to deliver a message to the people of Nineveh because the Ninevites were evil people. Jonah did not like the assignment, so he did not listen to God. Instead, he got in a boat that was headed in the opposite direction from Nineveh. Do you see yourself in this story? Have you thought that doing life your way was better than what God designed for you?

Jonah thought, if only he can get out of dodge he'll escape and get on with his life. So he got on a boat with a bunch of other dudes. Then God sent a violent storm that rocked the boat he was in. The other sailors on board were frantic! They wondered among themselves why God would do this to them. Once they realized that Jonah was on board and running from God, they had a rather good idea that he was the cause of the storm. They agreed to cast lots to see who had offended the gods and caused this terrible storm. The lot fell on Jonah. He was the culprit. Be careful whom you hang out with or whom you let on your boat. Is someone rocking your world? Take a look around; you may have to ask them to leave.

Then the sailors asked Jonah, "Why has this awful storm come down on us? Who are you? What is your line of work? What country are you from? What is your nationality?" (Jon. 1:8 [NLT]). They drilled Jonah for answers. They were angry that Jonah had selfishly put them in dire straits because of his sin. Jonah answered, "I am a Hebrew, and I worship the lord, the God of heaven who made the sea and the land." The sailors were terrified when they heard this, and he had already told them he was running away from the Lord. "Oh, why did you do it?" they groaned? (Jon. 1:9–10 [NLT]).

Sometimes, we pay the consequences for other people's sin or poor choices. Every day, innocent people die or are hurt by those who have selfish motives or agendas. Jonah told the sailors, "Throw me into the sea and it will become calm again." Instead, the sailors rowed even harder to get the ship to land. But the stormy sea was too violent for them, and they could not make it. Then they cried out to the Lord, Jonah's God. "Oh lord," they pleaded, "don't make us die for this man's sin. And don't hold us responsible for his death. O lord you have sent this storm upon him for your own good reasons." There was a purpose for the storm. "Then the sailors picked him up and threw him in the raging sea, and the storm stopped at once! The sailors were awestruck by the Lord's power, and they offered a sacrifice and vowed to serve him."

This story is often told about Jonah only. But there's a lot more to the story.

- God used the storm to get everyone's attention.
- Jonah took responsibility for his disobedience.
- God's power in calming the storm caused all the sailors on board to serve Him. It changed their hearts.
- God protected Jonah inside the fish because He was not finished with him.
- While inside the large fish, Jonah humbled himself and vowed to obey God.
- God gave Jonah a second chance to go to Nineveh, and Jonah obeyed.

- Jonah delivered the message from God with clarity and authority.
- The Ninevites' hearts were changed.

There was no escaping God! Jonah was swallowed up and lived inside the fish for three days and nights. Then Jonah prayed to the Lord from inside the fish. When you are all tangled up in seaweed and there's no escape route, it is a good time to pray. Jonah told God he would obey Him. God heard his prayer and ordered the fish to spit Jonah upon the beach. Sometimes, God has to take drastic measures to get our attention. Being trapped inside the belly of a fish for three days, the stench alone would be enough to make anyone surrender.

Unlike Secret Service agents, God can perform miracles. Once we capture the essence of who God is and understand the depth of His power and love, we will live differently. We will not run away from Him. We will not question His presence in our lives. We will choose our race wisely, always following the one who loves us most. There is nothing we can hide. We are fully exposed before a loving God who knows everything about us, and yet He loves us.

Another quality about God is that He will never force Himself on you. We must respond to His invitation to follow Him. If we disobey like Jonah did, he'll let us get all tangled up in our own mess. It wasn't until Jonah realized his own sin and fate that he turned to God. We do ourselves and our loved ones a big favor when we follow God. When we follow Him in obedience, we will not drag ourselves or others into unwanted places. We will not expose them to our consequences. The men and women of the Bible are so much like us. That is why it is so important to delve into the Word of God. We'll find ourselves in there. We will relate to the lives of the men and women who had temptations and struggles just like we do.

Jonah was stubborn and thought he had a better plan. David's brothers were jealous of their younger brother so much so that they were willing to take his life and lie about it. God had different plans for Jonah and David. He spared their lives, and they accomplished so much under the obedience and direction of God. God has the best plan for our lives, and yet many people still find a reason to run from Him. They ask,

- What will God require of me?
- What if He asked me to do something I do not want to do?
- Will I have to stop having fun?

- Will He put limits on my life?
- Will I have to stop … (fill in the blank)?
- Why do I need God when I am doing good without Him?

Oh my goodness, the excuses are countless! God just wants our hearts! Take all those questions and apply them to marriage.

- What will marriage require of me?
- What if my spouse gets a different job and we have to relocate and I do not want that for us?
- Will I have to give up all the fun I had in my single life?
- Will marriage put limits on me?
- Why do I need a spouse to be accountable to?

If we must ask these questions, then it should be a red flag for marriage. It is also a red flag for our perception of the Christian life. When we love someone, it is not a sacrifice; it's a partnership and a new way of life. It is easy to see the measure of our love if we have to ask these questions. Is God taking drastic measures to get our attention? Why does He bother to do that for us? Why does He stand and knock at the door of our hearts when over and over again He has been rejected, ignored, or shut out?

It comes down to two things, my friend:

1. **His omniscience** (He's all knowing). He has full access to our hearts and minds. He knows us! He knows our fears, our sins, our weaknesses, and our desire for independence. He knows everything about us, and yet He never gives up on us! He knows that if we keep doing life without Him, we will miss the greatest gift of all time—the gift of eternal life in heaven, the gift of His peace that passes all understanding, and so much more.

2. **He loves us!** His love runs deeper than our mortal minds can comprehend. We are fickle; He is not! We are subject to change; He is not! God's love is constant! He made the greatest sacrifice known to humanity. He gave His only Son to die on a rugged cross so that we would be set free from sin. His love runs deep, and when we turn and walk away from Him, as though He doesn't matter, we put another nail in His hand. He cries out to us, "Stop running away and run to Me!" Does anyone else love you that much?

Father God,

You lavish Your unconditional love upon me day after day. I am so undeserving of Your mercy and grace. Forgive me for taking the easy way out when You call me on an assignment. Forgive me for thinking my way is better than Your way. I surrender my life to You. Thank You for knowing me fully and yet loving me completely. I pray for Your peace that passes all my understanding as I walk with You. God, I need You!

In the name of my Lord and Savior,

Amen

CHAPTER 9

LEAVE YOUR PRIDE AT THE DOOR

Humility Is the Fear of the Lord

When pride comes, then comes disgrace,
but with humility comes wisdom.
—Proverbs 11:2

The LORD detests all the proud of heart. Be
sure of this: They will not go unpunished.
—Proverbs 16:5

Pride goes before destruction, a
haughty spirit before the fall.
—Proverbs 16:18

"Mommy, Mommy, look at me, aren't I beautiful?" Those
sweet words warm our hearts and make us chuckle when

they're said by a five-year-old who is all dressed up in her princess outfit. It is not so sweet to hear that kind of boasting when it is coming from someone far too old to be wearing a princess dress. If you are beautiful, you will not need to tell anyone because they will see it for themselves. Pride can be tricky. When we are successful, we want everyone to see what is going on that shows off our success, bigger homes, bigger cars, better toys. But how do we do that without making it so obvious? If I build a big enough house, it will represent our family well. If I post my world travels, my friends will be envious and see how well I am doing. If I am always posting about myself out having fun with lots of friends, people will see that I'm well-liked and popular. Nothing is wrong with having a big house, lots of friends, and being well traveled unless our motives are to impress others. No one can know the motives of another person. It is between us and God.

In this chapter, I am not talking about the kind of pride that is associated with our self-esteem or confidence. We should have that, and we should encourage and facilitate that quality in our children. The kind of pride I'm referring to leans more toward the puffed-up, boasting, arrogant and overconfident behavior that the Bible speaks against.

Destructive pride is nothing to be proud of. It's a gradual *slippery slope* that can happen over time. It can cause us to lose our grip on reality. We might find ourselves thinking more highly of ourselves than we should. Sometimes, it can be a blind spot in our lives that only others can see. There are moments we should celebrate, like an accomplishment, a goal, or milestone that has been achieved. These moments are worth celebrating. There is a big difference between being proud of something and living a pride-filled life. No one wakes up in the morning and says, "Today, I am going to be Polly Prideful." It is gradual, unintentional, and often a behavior that turns a wonderful person into someone no one wants to be around. That is why it's a very *slippery slope*.

In our culture, we have many avenues to keep ourselves healthy. We get dental exams, medical checkups, eye examinations, and wellness checkups. There's enough specialist to cover every area of our bodies from head to toe. If only we could find a "pride" consultant or get a prescription for humility, we would be all set. But then we might be too proud to go to the pharmacy to pick it up. And we would not want our friends or neighbors to see a script for humility sitting on our kitchen countertop. That would mean we have a pride problem.

Pride is such a *slippery slope*, and the antidote is not as simple as we think. We have heard about the downfall of many powerful people who allowed pride to control them. Those people are in the Bible too. Pharaoh was defiant. Saul was self-righteous. Jonah felt entitled. Eve was power hungry. Peter, the disciple, was overconfident. And those are just a few.

There are people like Lance Armstrong and Tom Brady, who ended their careers but felt compelled to return to the sport that dominated their life. Was it their pride? Pride not only is destructive to an individual but also has an impact on families, relationships, friends, teammates, and colleagues. Is it any wonder that God hates pride? "All who fear the Lord will hate evil. That is why I hate pride, arrogance, corruption, and perverted speech" (Prov. 8:13 [The Living Bible]).

Pride Offends God, and Pride Is a Sin against God

- Pride will not admit failure or sin.

The Bible says, "For all have sinned; and fall short of God's glorious standard" (Rom. 3:23 [The Living Bible]).

- Pride will not ask for help.

Jesus said, "Come to me, all of you who are weary and carry heavy burdens, and I will give you rest" (Matt. 11:28–30 [The Living Bible]).

- Pride is a mask that hides our full potential.

"For I know the plans I have for you," says the Lord. "They are plans for good and not for disaster, to give you a future and hope" (Jer. 29:11 [The Living Bible]).

Thus says the Lord, "Let not the wise man boast of his wisdom, let not the mighty man boast in his might, let not the rich man boast of his riches, but let him who boasts boast in this, that he understands, and knows me, that I am the Lord who practices steadfast love, justice, and righteousness in the earth. For in these things I delight, declares the Lord" (Jer. 9:23–24).

"15 Subtle Signs of Pride in Your Life," by Allen Parr

1. Assuming you already know something when someone is teaching
2. Seeing yourself as too good to perform certain tasks
3. Being too proud to ask for help
4. Feeling the need to consistently teach people things

5. Talking about yourself a lot
6. Thinking you are better than others who are different or less fortunate
7. When you disregard the advice of others
8. When you are consistently critical
9. Have a consistent need for attention and affirmation
10. Unable to receive constructive criticism
11. Overly obsessed with one's physical appearance
12. Unwilling to submit to authority
13. Ignoring people's attempt to communicate with you
14. Justifying your sin instead of admitting it
15. Name-dropping

If nothing strikes a chord with you, that should be a red flag because we all struggle with pride to a certain extent. The antidote for any shortcoming in our lives is to first acknowledge it, then confess it, then stop it. If we went to a physician with an addiction problem, the same steps would be required. Acknowledge it, confess it, and stop it. There may not be a prescription for humility or a pride consultant in our area. But the closer we walk with God, the more he will show us the areas of our lives that need to be worked on. That is the best prescription from the most reliable source.

Pride is ugly! It assumes more than it should. It hurts more than it realizes. It creates barriers that are hard to tear down. This is one of those topics that we all need to examine in our lives because *slippery slopes are slippery.* They slide right into our lives without an invitation. They can change us, stifle what is best for us, and ruin our reputation as a child of God. If you want to know anything, ask God, and He will find a way to reveal it to you.

Father God,

As I lay my head on my pillow tonight, comfort me with Your peace. When I wake up in the morning, guide me by Your truth. Help me to see those areas in my life that need to be changed. Open my eyes to the blind spots in my life that could hurt or offend others. Give me a spirit of humility so that I can represent You well in everything I do and say.

In Jesus's name,

Amen

CHAPTER 10

PERSONAL BLIND SPOTS

I Can See Clearly Now . . .

> Search me, O God and know my heart, test
> me and know my anxious thoughts. Point
> out anything in me that offends you, and
> lead me along the path of everlasting life.
> —Psalm 139:23–24 (King David)

It takes a brave heart to ask tough questions, and it takes humility to call on the God of the universe to point out anything that offends Him in our lives. It requires the laying down of our pride for honesty and self-examination. There is no one better to ask than our heavenly Father.

God knows us completely and loves us unconditionally! When we ask Him to identify those areas in our lives that can be painful to hear, He responds to us with love and grace. In the scripture above, King David is asking God to speak truth into his life. He knew he could trust his heavenly Father, who has unlimited vision and a heart full of love. It took courage for David to ask, and it takes courage for us to ask for God to point out our blind spots.

Blind spots are those areas in our character that others can see but we cannot. If a blind spot is not identified and addressed, it can keep us from living our best lives. It can cause misunderstandings and harm relationships.

Possible blind spots

- unusual amount of sarcasm or belittling
- fault finding
- excuses
- pride
- self-focus
- controlling behavior
- passive-aggressive behavior
- negativity
- manipulation
- fear that controls

When people become so comfortable with these habits that they lose sight of the impact it has on others, it becomes a blind spot in their lives that will destroy trust, character, and the respect that others have of them.

If you know someone that struggles in this area, then love them enough to talk with them in kindness and grace. If they accept your consolation, then they will have won your respect. If they become defensive and refuse to acknowledge your words, then you know that you've done your best to help them. We should never attempt to point out someone's blind spots until we ourselves have prayed for wisdom and guidance. It may not be our place.

Several years ago, our son, Jason, made a comment to me about a blind spot in my life. He said something along the line that I was playing life safe—that I wasn't being real or vulnerable. There's something about receiving feedback from one of your children that causes you to pause and reflect. Those words stayed with me, so I did some self-examination and found that he was probably right. Being real and vulnerable was hard for me. It can be hard to take risks.

After prayerful consideration, I was prompted to write my first book, *God's Perfect Strategy*. It's not a tell-all story because, frankly, that is between God and me. The book, however, is my best attempt to be real, vulnerable, and forthcoming. It is something I have to continue to work on. When you receive feedback that is sincere and it has your best interest at heart, that feedback can be a gift.

Blind spots can be subtle. They can be brought on by insecurities, a need to prove oneself, or an unhealthy need for acceptance. They can be harmful and cause misunderstandings. At the end of the day, we ask ourselves what kind of people we are striving to be. Is there a blind spot in my life that's keeping people at arm's length? Am I hindering my witness for God in any way?

King David had a heart that longed to be right with God. He was concerned about his character. Because of this, David was considered a man after God's own heart (1 Sam. 13:14). Blind spots are often about our internal character. When King David asked God to test him and lead him along the path of everlasting life, he wanted to be a godly man. It takes humility to follow. It is human nature to want to be in charge of our own lives. Sometimes, we even want to oversee other people's lives, but we all need guidance. No one has arrived. We are all still students learning how to be our best.

There are many examples in the Bible where God speaks to the blind spots in people's lives. When Jesus was teaching to the crowd about not judging other people, he said, "And why worry about a speck in your friend's eye when you have a log in your own." He went on to say, "How can you think of saying to your friend, 'Let me help you get rid of that speck in your eye,' when you can't see past the log in your own eye?" (Matt. 7:3–4 [NLT]). "You hypocrites, first take the log out of your own eye, and then you will see clearly to take the speck out of your brother's eye" (Matt. 7:5 [ESV]).

The people that Jesus is speaking to in the crowd could only see the problem in their friend's life. Jesus frankly points out to them that their own problem is much bigger than those they are accusing. We cannot help anyone until our own lives are in order. Another example from the Bible comes from a story about Simon Peter, one of Jesus's closest disciples. Peter would do anything for Jesus. He loved Him, he followed Him, and he trusted in Him. But Peter had a blind spot in his life. On the way to the Mount of Olives, Jesus told his disciples, "Tonight, all of you will desert me. For the Scriptures say, 'God will strike the Shepherd, and the sheep of the flock will be scattered'" (Matt. 26:31 [NLT]).

Peter declared to Jesus, "Even if everyone else deserts you, I will never desert you." Jesus replied, "I tell you the truth, Peter, this very night, before the rooster crows, you will deny three times that you know me." "No, Peter insisted. Even if I have to die with you, I will never deny you!" And all the disciples vowed the same (Matt. 26:33–35 [NLT]).

You see, Peter didn't understand his own fears and weaknesses. He was certain and confident that he could never deny knowing the one who came to be the Savior of the world. Jesus was his friend, his teacher, and, above all, his Lord. But when Peter was faced with his own fate, he vehemently denied Jesus over and over again. He didn't want to be associated with the man they were about to crucify.

Peter was sitting outside in the courtyard. A servant girl came over and said to him, "You were one of those with Jesus the Galilean." But Peter denied it in front of everyone. "I don't know what you are talking about," he said (Matt. 26:70 [NLT]).

Later, out by the gate, another servant girl noticed him and said to those standing around. "This man was with Jesus of Nazareth." Again Peter denied it, this time with an oath. "I don't even know the man," he said (Matt. 26:71 [NLT]).

A little later, some of the other bystanders came over to Peter and said, "You must be one of them; we can tell by your Galilean accent." Peter swore, "A curse on me if I'm lying—I don't know the man!" (Matt. 26:73–74 [NLT]).

And, immediately, the rooster crowed. Suddenly, Jesus's words flashed through Peter's mind: "Before the rooster crows, you will deny knowing me three times." And Peter went away, weeping bitterly (Matt. 26:75 [NLT]).

It must have been the saddest day of Peter's life. As I've studied this story, I'm struck with the question, "Is my behavior dependent on whom I am with, or is my behavior dependent on whom I belong to? Am I consistent? In Peter's case, he was super confident as long as he was with Jesus. But when Peter got outside of his safe place, he became a different person. Peter could not even imagine disowning Christ. Is that a blind spot or what?

Jesus, the Son of God, in His grace and mercy, forgave Peter for denying Him. God knew Peter better than Peter knew himself. The same is true for us. God knows our blind spots. He knows everything about us. So, when we approach God as David did and ask him to search our hearts, He will! He will reveal the log in our eye so that we can accomplish his purpose. Honesty is nothing to be afraid of; it is something we should all long for.

God is in the business of developing people to be used for His glory. And any *slippery slope* that interferes with our growth as children of God will keep us as spiritual preemies. We live in a world that desperately needs men and women who will live unashamed for God's sake and future generations. We are called to stand firm!

We have looked at a couple of examples from the Bible, but now let us bring it home. One of the most frightening blind spots in our culture today is watching parents or loved ones set a poor example for their children. A good parent, teacher, or loved one *would never intentionally* set a poor example for someone under their care.

Joyce Meyer, of Joyce Meyer Ministries, says it so well. She said that God pointed out to her early on in her ministry that "as many people that she can help is the same number of people that she can hurt."

Our blind spots can hurt people. We cannot expect our children to be respectful when we're not respectful. We cannot expect our children to not be racist when we act like anyone different from us is to be feared. We cannot expect our children to be kind when we make fun of people or laugh about things a person has no control over. As believers, we must set the example because the world, and culture, is failing our children big time! Our children and grandchildren are watching us. They desperately need good and consistent examples.

Take a minute today and be honest. Ask yourself, "Who or what is it that is influencing my life? Is it God, or is it wealth, politics, culture, power, popularity, or social media? Is it my drive for success? Is it my image? Do I have something to prove? What drives me and leads me?" God does not want competition with our lives. He wants all of us. He deserves to have all of us!

King David did not go to his parents to ask them to search his heart. He didn't go to Bathsheba, the woman he had an affair with, and asked her to search his heart. He went to the only living God and poured out his humble heart. When we want real answers, we go to the God of truth. Too many times we are afraid of truth, but it is truth that will set us free.

This is a prayer we need to pray often. It is not a one-and-done prayer. We are constantly being bombarded by the influences of our culture so harmful attitudes can creep into our hearts and minds and show up in our words and behaviors. It happens often and can easily become more of our nature than we want it to be. It's a very slippery slope.

At the end of the day, we need to be like David and pray, "Search me, O God and know my heart, test me and know my anxious thoughts. Point out anything in me that offends you and lead me along the path of everlasting life" (Ps. 139:23–24 [King David]). When we fully understand the love of God, we will trust him from the depths of our hearts.

Father God,

As I put this chapter to rest, I am reminded of Your holiness, purity, and sovereignty. I am reminded of Your grace and mercy. I am reminded that You created me for a purpose, and if I want that purpose to be fulfilled, I must trust You and walk with You.

Search my heart, oh God, and identify the areas of my character that I need to change. Forgive me for the sin of pride, selfishness, judgment, and harmful motives that lead to destruction. I want to follow You all the days of my life. Let my life be an example of Your love and grace.

In Jesus's name,

Amen

CHAPTER 11

WAIT A MINUTE! I CAN FIX THAT!

Stay Out of God's Workshop!

But now, O LORD, you are our Father;
we are the clay, and you are the potter;
we are all the work of your hand.
—Isaiah 64:8 (ESV)

This is my toughest *slippery slope*! I hate to admit it, but it is true. I'm a fixer. Give me a problem, anybody's problem, and I will try to fix it. How foolish! I have often learned the hard way—to wait upon the Lord. Don't get me wrong; if we see an immediate need and can meet that need, I believe we should. However, for me, it was much deeper than that. I not only wanted to fix the problem but also wanted to fix the person.

Have you ever thought, *If only they would do this or that, their problem would be solved?* Or, *I wish so-and-so would have heard that message—that is exactly what they needed to hear?* How about this one: *If only they would just listen to me?* If we are not careful, we can put ourselves in the potter's workshop and become an interference more than a help.

Recently, I was having my quiet time and praying for someone whom I thought had a problem, and at the same time, I was hinting to God at how I thought He could fix the problem. Suddenly, I felt in my spirit God saying to me, "Stay out of my workshop!" That was humbling and much needed. Who am I to tell the Potter how to form the clay?

If you are a fixer, you know what I'm talking about. The bad news is that we can't fix anyone! The good news is we can't fix anyone! Whatever quick fix we can produce is a poor choice in comparisons to God's plan. We need to get out of His way unless He calls us to do otherwise.

Our culture invokes high-speed everything: high-speed internet, high-speed rail. We want to get where we're going and get information as fast as possible. We are a hurry-up-and-get-it-done society. God does not work that way! He is never in a hurry, and that can be frustrating for some of us. I used to get impatient with slow drivers; now I am one. When you are retired, there is no need to hurry. You have forty more hours in a week than you had when you worked full time. Slow down and savor the moment. Slowing down is not easy, especially when you are used to going full speed ahead.

Listen to King David's plea for help.

Psalms 13 1–6, "O lord, how long will you forget me? Forever? How long will you look the other way? How long must I struggle with anguish in my soul, with sorrow in my heart, every day? How long will my enemy have the upper hand? Turn and answer me, O lord my God! Restore the sparkle in my eyes, or I will die. Don't let my enemies gloat, saying, 'We have defeated him!' Don't let them rejoice at my downfall. *But I trust in your unfailing love, I will rejoice because you have rescued me. I will sing to the lord because he is good to me.*"

When we go to the Lord and earnestly seek Him for ourselves or others, we need to leave it in His workshop. We are to call upon the name of the Lord. But nowhere does it say to call upon the name of the Lord and leave a message with advice.

I love how David ended his prayer in Psalm 13. After he ranted and raved and questioned God several times about his whereabouts, David concludes by saying, "But I trust in your unfailing love, I will rejoice because you have rescued me. I will sing to the lord because he is good to me."

The bottom line is God wants our trust and obedience. We have no idea what is going on in the workshop, and we have no clue how much chiseling is required to reshape the clay. Sometimes, it takes months, and other times it takes years or a lifetime for someone to submit to the chiseling. Some people never do.

For someone who cares deeply about people and only wants the best for them, we can do ourselves a big favor by modeling David's prayer, "But I trust in your unfailing love." When we are told to stay out of the workshop, we need to trust in God's timing.

When we jump in and try to fix something that isn't ours to fix, we can be interfering in God's plan. I do not want that on my conscience, do you? Instead, I would rather be persistent in prayer and faithful to let God do His work. I am going to continue to be tempted to fix what isn't mine to fix, to change what is not mine to change. God does not want us sitting back doing nothing. When God invites us to be become involved with Him in His work, then we should respond willingly.

Recently, our pastor shared an analogy about a stained glass window. He displayed a picture of hundreds of broken pieces of glass. They were beautiful chips of different colors but with no purpose. He talked about the tedious hours it takes to form a beautiful picture with those broken pieces. The same is true for a potter. They start with a ball of clay and start by shaping it with their hands and fingers. They use many different tools to get the item just the way they want it. The clay goes through many changes until it is ready for use. That is how God is with us. He molds us and shapes us for His glory. Sometimes, it is painful. But instead of interfering with the Potter, trust His timing and His process. The blueprint He has for our lives and the life of our loved ones is in progress. When it's completed, it will be beautiful.

The serenity prayer says it perfectly.

"Lord grant me the strength to accept the things I cannot change, the courage to change the things I can, and wisdom to know the difference" (Reinhold Niebuhr).

CHAPTER 12

PUT ON THE FINAL TOUCHES

Prepare for the Upgrade

No eye has seen, no ear has heard, and
no mind has imagined what God has
prepared for those who love him.
—1 Corinthians 2:9 (NLT)

The internet leaves little to the imagination. By the time we get ready to depart for vacation, we know what our condominium will look like, the surrounding area that we will be staying in, and even the seats we are assigned on the airplane. Researching is important so the destination meets our expectations, but it leaves no element of surprise.

Traveling was much different when I was a kid. My dad would spend time charting out our course from a paper map of the United States. There was no GPS. My parents packed our suitcases, loaded up the car, and off we went, Mom and Dad in the front and us three kids in the backseat. No SUV! We would find a motel when Dad was too tired to drive anymore. If we were lucky, the motel had a pool. But no matter where we went, it was a surprise for all of us.

There is no preview of heaven. You will not find any pictures on the internet. There is nothing published in *Traveler* magazine or *Destinations of a Lifetime*. As beautiful and enticing as some of those places are, heaven is so much better!

Our minds cannot begin to comprehend the sights, the sounds, the luxuries, the adventures, the relationships that God has planned for us. The Bible says, "That no eye has seen, no ear has heard, and no mind can imagine what He has prepared for us!" I'm super excited about that, and you should be too! When a believer dies, it is a transition. There is no packing, preparation, cost involved, or maps. There is no GPS or airport delays for our trip to heaven. That sounds wonderful to me!

One thing most airports have in common is a moving walkway. If we are in a hurry or want to rest our legs, we can step on the walkway, and it will take us down a long corridor toward our terminal. It is very convenient. All we need to do is stand still, and the large conveyer belt will propel us forward. Life is much like is a moving walkway. Even when we are just standing or sitting around doing nothing, the clock is ticking and life is moving. We cannot get off in the middle of a moving walkway; it just doesn't work that way. Time doesn't stand still either. We cannot stop the clock.

Every moving walkway has an end to it, a place to step off. Such is life. God knows exactly when our personal walkway will end. The Bible says, "Make the most of every chance you get. These are desperate times" (Eph. 5:16 [The Message]). When we are traveling, there is nothing better than getting a free upgrade. Maybe it is a better seat on an airplane, a bigger condominium for the same price, or a beach-front hotel room. It is a bonus when things work out that way. No matter what stage of life you are in, God wants us to know there is an upgrade coming. He is planning a home for us that will knock our socks off. All we have to do is accept His invitation. It's eternal, it's valuable, and it's free!

But we must never forget that someone paid for the move. Someone made a way for us to go to heaven. It came with a high price! All our sins and imperfections that would keep us out of a perfect heaven were nailed through the hands and feet of Jesus. He invites us to His home, but we cannot go if we do not believe or if we do not accept His invitation. He wants us! He wants all of us!

So, how do we prepare for the move? Get rid of all the junk. Whenever we hang on to too much bad stuff, it occupies space that could be used for something better. It always feels good to lighten the load. Examine every slippery slope because, if left unattended, they can propel us to places we never intended to go. They are our battles!

The good news is we can have the Storm Changer, the God of Angel Armies, in our corner if we want to, or we can do it all by ourselves. There is an antidote for every slippery slope, and His name is Jesus! When Jesus walked the earth, He had one calling, and that was to honor and glorify His heavenly Father. Our calling is the same. As we honor God, we will find ourselves moving in the right direction. There is no need to complicate things. There is no place for *slippery slopes* in our new heavenly home. It will be perfect, and we will be transformed!

Ask God to help you become aware of the *slippery slopes* in your life. Ask Him to give you a passion for what matters to Him. He will! He loves us too much not to answer a sincere call for help. No one else loves us that much! While we wait, we put on the final touches. We get rid of all the junk in our lives because there is a party, a feast waiting for us. It is the best invitation we will ever get. All we need to do is accept the invitation. "Finally, brothers rejoice. Aim for restoration, comfort one another, agree with one another, live in peace; and the God of love and peace will be with you" (2 Cor. 13:11).

Father God,

I want to thank You for using my mistakes to make me better. I want to thank You for protecting me through the storms of life. I thank You for forgiving me and allowing me to call You Dad!

I'm so excited for heaven that I want to take as many people with me as possible! My prayer is that You will give me wisdom to represent You well so that I will never be a hindrance to anyone. Help me to spot evil and run from it. Help me to run with open arms to the opportunities You put in my path.

Father, I love being with my husband and family. I enjoy the opportunities that You have given us here on earth.

But nothing in all creation will compare to the home You have prepared for us. Father, while we wait, open the hearts of those yet to accept You as Lord. Change every stubborn and pride-filled heart. Give understanding to those who genuinely want to follow You. Draw those who are running away back into Your fold.

Clear our clouded vision. Chisel away the slippery slopes in our lives that leave us feeling tired, anxious, fragile, and incomplete. Develop us into the people You desire us to be. You are the antidote that we so desperately need. Thank You, Lord, for being the best Dad a girl could ever ask for. I can't wait to see You in person.

I love You,

Karen

NOTES

1. Corrie Ten Boom,
   https://www.amightygirl.com/blog?p=23970.

2. Chase Culbertson, Newspring Church,
   https://newspring.cc/articles/3-ways-christianity-is-different-from-other-religions.

3. Stephanie Larratt, Today all day, "It's Scary to Be Vulnerable,"
   https://www.today.com/tmrw/overcoming-fear-celebsshare-inspiring-stories-about-overcoming-feart173976.

4. Leo Strobel, *The Case for Christ*.

5. Allen Parr Ministries, "15 Subtle Signs of Pride in Your Life,"
allenparr.com.

6. Dave Lescalleet, Pruitt Cares Foundation, "What God Hates,"
pruittcares.org.

Printed in the United States
by Baker & Taylor Publisher Services